A PROPHECY FULFILLED

THE STORY OF CLARENCE T.C. CHING

Mr. and Mrs. Clarence T.C. Ching

A PROPHECY FULFILLED

THE STORY OF CLARENCE T.C. CHING

Lance Tominaga

WATERMARK
PUBLISHING

© 2009 The Clarence T.C. Ching Foundation

ISBN 978-0-9821698-8-9

Library of Congress Control Number: 2009937467

Design and production
Marisa Oshiro, Osaki Creative Group

Photography
Hawai'i State Archives, p. 30
Olivier Koning, p. 90 (top)
All other photos used with permission of the Clarence T.C. Ching
family, *The Honolulu Advertiser*, the Palolo Chinese Home
(p.87 bottom), and beneficiary schools (pp. 84-90).

Watermark Publishing
1088 Bishop Street, Suite 310
Honolulu, Hawai'i 96813
www.bookshawaii.net

A publication of
The Clarence T.C. Ching Foundation
1001 Bishop Street, Suite 960
Honolulu, Hawai'i 96813

Printed in China

*This book was commissioned by The Clarence T.C. Ching Foundation
in loving memory of Clarence T.C. Ching.*

CONTENTS

FOREWORD

BY RAYMOND J. TAM

We were ecstatic and jumping with joy when my mother announced that her brother Clarence had gifted her with a portion of his sizable estate. We knew that Mom had played a prominent role in raising Clarence and her other nine siblings. As the oldest daughter, she had become a surrogate mother to the other children because her mother (my grandmother) had tiny, bound feet—fashionable in China at that time, and considered beautiful, "upper class" and even sexy. Women with big feet were considered to be of peasant stock and destined to work in the fields. Ladies with tiny, bound feet were regarded as "high society." They were to be waited upon, because they were so dainty and clearly could not perform heavy labor in the fields. And, while my grandmother had no difficulty birthing eleven babies, she could not physically manage the care of this large brood of active children. Thus, the task of rearing her ten siblings fell to my mother, and the choice of my mother as a beneficiary of Uncle Clarence's largesse was understandable.

But we were flabbergasted and dumbfounded when my mother then told us that he had not only gifted her with a portion of his estate; he had also given a percentage interest to his other nine brothers and sisters!

Then we heard with astonishment, our mouths wide open, that not only had he given part of his estate to his own brothers and sisters; he had also given a percentage interest to each of his wife's nine brothers and sisters

Ten brothers and sisters, plus nine brothers and sisters of Aunty Dot—a total of nineteen beneficiaries! What manner of man was this? Who in his right mind would share his good fortune with not one, not two, not three—but *nineteen* siblings and in-laws? And he was still in his 40s—in the prime of his life! For the life of me, I could not figure him out. Either he had been drinking a lot of '*ōkolehao* or he was the most generous, caring family man in Hawai'i.

I knew that my grandparents had come from the old country, that they were strict Buddhists and had raised their children with Confucian ideals and principles. Later, I learned that Uncle Clarence had been a very frail and sickly child, and I learned about the "prophecy of greatness" made in Anahola, Kaua'i, by my grandfather. I knew that the family had sacrificed to send Uncle Clarence from Kaua'i to

Honolulu to attend Saint Louis School. I learned that Clarence Ching was a model student, that he was twice-elected President of his class and that he was a champion boxer. A Saint Louis graduate myself, I knew that the school's motto, *Mindful and Faithful* (mindful of others and faithful to Christian values and ideals), would have been solidly instilled in him. I also knew that he would have been steadfastly taught the Saint Louis School creed by the Marianist Brothers: "Faith, Hope and Charity— the greatest of which is Charity."

After his wondrous gifts to his family, Clarence Ching continued his largesse. As President of the Chinese Chamber of Commerce, he recognized that the Chinese community had no center or meeting place to assemble and congregate. With the help of dedicated townspeople, he organized and led the development of the block-long Chinese Cultural Plaza. When they wanted to name the Plaza after him, he humbly refused, telling his associates that the Plaza was built not for his ego but for the entire Chinese community.

Then came the magnificent gift to the people of Hawai'i: KUKUI GARDENS.

In 1966, the Honolulu Redevelopment Agency sought someone or some organization to develop more than nineteen acres of land in downtown Honolulu. From King Street *mauka* to Vineyard Boulevard and from Liliha Street to A'ala Street, this was a huge parcel of land made available for low-cost, affordable housing.

Clarence Ching decided to go for it. He sought out the best architectural firm in the U.S. He learned that the architectural firm of Daniel, Mann, Johnson & Mendenhall enjoyed a commanding reputation as one of the finest in the land. They were not cheap, but they were the best. He contacted and eventually hired them. Clarence was there to win the bid—and he spared no expense. By a fortuitous happenstance, Daniel, Mann, Johnson & Mendenhall assigned the design task to a rising, budding young architect named César Pelli, whose career would endure for more than 45 years and who is today renowned as an architectural genius and an international superstar.

Clarence's competition was a non-profit organization made up of companies from management, several labor unions and the Honolulu Council of Churches. They were formidable adversaries, and they, too, went all-out to win the bid.

But César Pelli's brilliant design, together with Clarence's reputation as a proven successful developer, won the day. The contract was awarded to The Clarence T.C. Ching Foundation.

A total of 822 apartment units were built on the 19.5 acres of land. And if you compare them to their Mayor Wright Housing neighbor across the street, you can really appreciate the genius of César Pelli.

In César Pelli's own words: "I have the warmest memories of working for Clarence Ching in the design of Kukui Gardens. Mr. Ching was very bright, clear-headed, and he told me exactly what he wanted; but he gave me a free hand in making design decisions. The Kukui Gardens was very much liked by everyone who lived there. They felt the units were more like homes and not apartments. It is still one of my favorite projects."

But why did Clarence T.C. Ching want to develop Kukui Gardens so badly?

There was little opportunity for profit, since rental rates would be controlled by the U.S. Department of Housing and Urban Development and would therefore be extremely low. What is more, until the 40-year mortgage was paid off, there would be no viable market for resale. In addition, a sizable down payment from the highest bidder was required. But Clarence Ching was not deterred. He seeded the project, and the rest is history.

Other than a small, obscure plaque bearing the name "The Clarence T.C. Ching Foundation," which was nailed to a tree—and subsequently removed—Clarence Ching's name does not appear at Kukui Gardens. Anywhere! One amazing part of this magnificent man's story is how he shunned publicity. It is not Clarence Ching Gardens. Or Clarence Ching Kukui Gardens. It is simply Kukui Gardens.

And not only that: *He gave it all away! The whole works! He donated Kukui Gardens to charity!* To The Clarence T.C. Ching Foundation, a 501(c)(3) non-profit organization. So that any profits from rental income or any appreciation from the resale of the property would be used solely to help the poor, the needy and other worthy charitable causes in Hawai'i. Unbelievable!

Clarence Ching did not develop the Kukui Gardens project for personal glory or riches for himself, his family, relatives or investors. He was not looking for personal profit or appreciation from resale. Rather, he had an insatiable desire to give back to the people of Hawai'i. To his people. To help those in need. To show his gratitude to Hawai'i for the wonderful support and encouragement he received to allow him to achieve his lifetime accomplishments. He spent hundreds of thousands of dollars of his own money to build the project, worked diligently to develop the huge complex, and then, when all was said and done, donated the entire 19.5 acres and 822 apartment units to charity! *What an amazing, unbelievable, unique, humane human being!*

In the book *Confucius, a Philosopher for the Ages*, author Xu Yuanxiang writes that Confucius, who lived from 551 to 479 B.C., espoused the concept of *Ren*. When one of his disciples asked Confucius, "Master, what is the exact meaning of *Ren*?" Confucius answered, "Loving people. You should love people; love others." He explained that this concept of benevolence is inherent in one's inner self, that it is insufficient to love only your relatives and show filial piety to your parents, that one should expand this love to the extent of loving all people under Heaven—and that only by doing this could one earn the description of exhibiting the qualities of *Ren*.

And then I understood.

My grandparents were Buddhists, and they raised their family with an emphasis on Confucian principles and ideals. The concept of *Ren*.

And as I said, Clarence Ching had been taught at Saint Louis School, by the Marianist Brothers, "Faith, Hope and Charity—the greatest of which is Charity."

His personal creed was a combination of Confucianism and Christianity. *Ren* and Charity. What a winning combination!

Clarence T.C. Ching stands as a shining beacon of generosity and love—a compassionate humanitarian for the ages.

Raymond Tam is an attorney practicing in Honolulu, Hawai'i. He is a nephew of Clarence T.C. Ching and a Trustee and Vice Chairman of The Clarence T.C. Ching Foundation.

INTRODUCTION
THE PROPHECY

He was a frail and sickly boy. His rail-thin frame and frequent bouts of illness were causes of deep concern. There were times when his family wondered if he would even live to see his teenage years.

Undeterred, his father made a bold prediction: "If he survives, he will become an important, prosperous and outstanding man, and he will help the rest of our family."

Clarence T.C. Ching not only survived; he went on to fulfill his father's remarkable prophecy. In fact, the elder Ching could not have imagined just how "important, prosperous and outstanding" young Clarence would become.

The story of Clarence Ching is as unlikely as it is inspiring. His is a true rags-to-riches tale, created from equal parts destiny and roll-up-your-sleeves hard work. It was destiny, after all, that provided him a chance meeting with an old friend from the Damon Tract neighborhood—an encounter that led Ching, along with a Saint Louis School classmate, to develop one of O‘ahu's most promising pieces of real estate. Yet Clarence Ching was also the embodiment of the self-made man, a tireless, ambitious and driven Horatio Alger of the Hawaiian Islands.

What makes Clarence Ching's life and legacy so compelling?

He was very poor as a child, but he earned enough wealth to help his family and thousands of Hawai‘i residents.

He was feeble and ailing, yet one day he became a boxing champion.

He never earned a college degree, but he was so successful and held in such high regard that he advised some of the most prominent movers and shakers in Hawai‘i, including Gov. John A. Burns and Mayor Neal S. Blaisdell.

Clarence Ching's career portfolio included ventures in land development, real estate, insurance, banking and construction. When it became clear that his development projects were going to be a success, he contacted his ten brothers and sisters, as well as his wife's nine siblings, and deeded each of them a portion of these developments.

"With a stroke of a pen, he fulfilled his father's prediction," noted his nephew, Raymond Tam.

But the story does not end there. Appreciative of his Chinese heritage, Ching was President of the Sun Yat-sen School, President of the Chinese Chamber of Commerce and President of the Ching Clan Society. When he saw the need for a central meeting place for local Chinese, Ching helped develop an entire city block in downtown Honolulu's historic Chinatown, including a three-story centerpiece called the Chinese Cultural Plaza.

Ultimately, Ching sought to help people of all races and backgrounds, particularly those who faced the kind of financial hardships that his family had experienced when he was growing up on the island of Kaua'i. In the late 1960s, he formed the non-profit Clarence T.C. Ching Foundation as a vehicle to purchase 19.5 acres in downtown Honolulu. There he built Kukui Gardens, his 822-unit apartment complex for low-income residents.

"The best part about Kukui Gardens? He donated all the money from the project to charity, through his Foundation," Raymond Tam pointed out. "That is just the kind of person he was. Think about it. He did not have to do it. He did not make a dime from Kukui Gardens. How many other successful businessmen would undertake such a project? His generosity and caring for the community made him special."

A quarter-century after his death in 1985, detailed biographical information and personal insights about Clarence Ching are not easy to find. Many of his contemporaries and peers—those who knew him best—have also passed on. More important, he was, despite his impressive résumé, a humble local boy who never liked to bask in the glow of his achievements. Instead, he took pains to avoid the limelight, preferring to let others take credit for his successes.

"He was a very modest person," recalled Cathy Ching, a granddaughter and Trustee of The Clarence T.C. Ching Foundation. "He was never the type of person to toot his own horn and say, 'Look at all the great things I did.'"

Amongst his more public successes, Ching never forgot his family and friends. Gene Tiwanak, a friend and colleague who worked with Ching for some twelve years, told this story to illustrate: "Clarence loved golf, and he always played in our medical staff's golf tournament. In 1975 or '76, I happened to be his partner. At the time, I had just started learning to play. But these doctors liked to bet. So because I did not play very often, they agreed to bet small, something like $2 a hole. I figured, well, this is okay. The most I can lose is a few dollars.

"Well, every time no one wins a hole, it is a 'push,' which means the next hole is double or nothing. So when we got to the 18th hole, one of the doctors said, 'Clarence, you are down. How about double or nothing?' And Clarence asked, 'How much are we down?' It turned out we were down 68 bucks. If we lost the hole, I would have owed $136! I was really spooked, especially since I only had a few dollars on me."

Ching won the hole for his team, then turned to Tiwanak and smiled, "Was tough, eh? No worry; I would have taken care of you."

That was Clarence Ching: a leader who could be counted on when needed, a competitor who thrived in adverse situations and, in the end, a philanthropist who took immense joy in taking care of people.

Perhaps Dorothy Tam Ching, Clarence Ching's niece and longtime secretary, said it best: "He was a hardworking and caring businessman who wanted to help the less fortunate and give back to the community. And that is what he did. Even after he became very successful, he never forgot his roots.

"I feel that he was just destined to do something great." ❧

CHAPTER ONE
HUMBLE
BEGINNINGS

HUMBLE BEGINNINGS

Clarence Thing Chock Ching was born on June 2, 1912, in Anahola, Kaua'i. He entered a world in rapid transition. Earlier in the year, the Republic of China was established, with Dr. Sun Yat-sen elected as its first provisional President. In the United States, New Mexico and Arizona were admitted as the 47th and 48th states of the Union. Locally, Duke Kahanamoku was regaled as Hawai'i's first Olympic gold medalist, having won the 100-meter freestyle swimming event in Stockholm, Sweden. And much of the world was still reeling from the events of April 14, when the "unsinkable" *Titanic*, then the largest passenger steamship in the world, struck an iceberg on her maiden voyage, sinking and killing 1,517 passengers and crewmembers.

Of course, little of this mattered to Ching Koon Hook and his wife, Kam Sing. All they knew was that they had a beautiful new addition to their growing family.

A modest community on Kaua'i's scenic north shore, Anahola in 1912 was primarily an agricultural area inhabited by farmers and plantation workers. It is said that Anahola was named after a *mo'o*, a lizard that took the form of a human on land and, in the ocean, that of a merman.

Ching Hook grew up in the village of Hung Mee, a suburb of the city of Nam Long in the See Dai Doo area in the Kwangtung province of southern China. As a teenager, he heard tales of a group of tropical Pacific islands known as Tan Heung San, where workers could earn great wealth for a few years of labor.

In her 1977 biography of Ching Hook, *Ching Hook from Hung Mee*, Francis Lai Ching wrote: "Thousands of Chinese had already answered this call and gone to this wondrous land in the quest for a better future. A number of Hung Mee villagers had returned after their contracts were up with enough money to build themselves houses that were an envy to all their neighbors. Tan Heung San was such a good place that out of every two men who went there to work, usually one chose to remain to spend the rest of his days."

Tan Heung San, or Land of the Sandalwood, was what the Chinese called Hawai'i.

Lured by this promise of a better life, Ching Hook and his youngest brother,

Ching Kau, left Hung Mee in 1881. After a seven-week journey across the sea, they landed at Honolulu Harbor, where the elder sibling learned to introduce himself by simply saying, "Ching Hook from Hung Mee, Canton, China."

A few days later, the brothers set sail for Kaua'i, where they found work as rice planters in Anahola. It was a difficult life toiling in the rice paddies, but they were excellent workers. In time, Ching Hook saved enough money to purchase several acres of land next to the mountains. A large stream adjoined the property, and his nearest neighbor was three miles away. Later, Ching Hook also bought a rice mill. All the farmers used his rice mill, as it was the only one in the area. For Ching Hook and Ching Kau, life on Kaua'i was good.

Hee Kam Sing, meanwhile, arrived in Hawai'i from China in 1887, when she was only six years old. Wrote Francis Lai Ching, "She was brought up in the old Chinese traditions and religion to be a good wife and mother. She was taught to be gentle, obedient and submissive. Kam Sing was an attractive girl with a longish oval face. She was five feet and three inches tall and walked on small bound feet." (At the time, foot binding was a long-practiced Chinese custom, one viewed as a status symbol for women. The custom was banned in China in the early 20th century.)

Ching Hook and Kam Sing were married in 1898 in a traditional Chinese ceremony. Over time, the couple would have eleven children: T.F. (Thing Fai), Chow (Thing Chow), Mae (Yuk Cue), Mildred (Yuk Ngan), Clarence (Thing Chock), Clifford (Thing Fong), Myrtle (Yuk Sun), Bernard (Thing Chan), twins Gilbert (Thing Chee) and Herbert (Thing Yuk), and Leonard (Thing Quon). All were born in Anahola except for the youngest, Leonard, who was born after the family had moved to Honolulu.

"Our parents were strict, but they never raised their voices or anything like that," recalled Myrtle Ching, the youngest daughter. "You just had to do what they told you to do. You never answered back."

Anahola was an ideal place to raise children. The young adventurers would explore the nearby mountains, going on hiking excursions and picking wild fruit such as guavas, mountain apples, bananas, mangoes, passion fruit and an assortment of berries. Freshwater streams were full of minnows and crayfish to catch.

However, recreation time was a rare luxury for Ching Hook's children, who learned the value of hard work at a very early age. The boys helped their father in the fields and with any other outdoor chores. The girls helped their mother with the housekeeping and tending to the younger kids.

"Because of her small bound feet Kam Sing did not do any work outside of her house," wrote Francis Lai Ching. "In order to do the family washing, her older boys T.F. and Chow hauled buckets of water for her. When Mae and Mildred were old enough, they did the laundry in the cool mountain stream, using river rocks to help them scrub the pieces that were heavily soiled. The girls always found this a very pleasant chore, for it was cool and refreshing at the stream. There was something very fascinating and relaxing to watch and listen to the gurgling water."

Without a doubt, Clarence Ching's "workaholic" ways can be traced to his childhood. His parents instilled a strong work ethic in him, and he, in turn, would pass it on to his own children and grandchildren.

"We made our kids work, too," said Frances "Mimi" Ching, wife of Clarence's oldest son, Lawrence. "As soon as they were fifteen, they would go get their work permit and find something to do. They never sat around. My father-in-law always instilled that value of hard work. My kids respected him because they saw how hard he worked."

"He provided enough to his family so that we would be comfortable," said granddaughter Cathy, "but not to the point where we did not need to work. It is not like we could just live off a trust. I think that was a smart move. I have seen instances where people have too much money handed to them."

In Clarence's early years, there was no running water or electricity. Cold water from the stream was poured into a big metal tub, and heated water was added to make the temperature bearable. In the evening, kerosene lamps were lit and hung on hooks from the ceiling.

The family raised their own livestock, caught fish from the streams and harvested vegetables from their gardens. Chickens were kept for both meat and eggs. The family kept very few ducks, however, because the waterfowl would often escape to the rice paddies and eat the rice. When a pig was slaughtered, the entire family feasted on fresh pork for two days, and any leftover meat was salted for later use.

"Even after we moved to Honolulu, our parents would buy our chickens and ducks live," said Herbert Ching, one of the youngest of Ching Hook and Kam Sing's eight sons. "They would bring a chicken home, and we would butcher it. I remember that my mother could never bring herself to kill the chicken. It was up to the boys to do it."

In *Ching Hook from Hung Mee*, the author described how the family often caught mullet and *āholehole* from the mountain stream: "Ching Hook would take his boys and girls up the stream until they found a school of fish. Then he instructed them to pick up river pebbles and throw them just behind the school. Everyone would take part with great enthusiasm and run along the side of the stream excitedly throwing river rocks to chase the fish downstream into their trap. Cornered in the trap, the fish would leap up and down trying desperately to escape while everyone would joyfully catch the fish to fill their baskets."

The family went through their share of hard times. An especially painful tragedy occurred shortly before Ching Hook decided to move his family to Honolulu.

Francis Lai Ching wrote: "For days dark nimbus clouds had built up in the mountains above their farm until they hung like a dark grey veil overhead. Then, as if from an angry monster in the sky, lightning flashed and thunder roared incessantly while violent rains in a solid wall of water came down on the mountains of Anahola! By the time the water reached the lower land, it had gained such momentum that it swept everything—buildings, people, livestock, trees, plants and rice fields—in its path out into the sea."

Fortunately, Ching Hook's home and livestock were on higher ground, so they were spared. While he did lose his rice fields and garden, he knew they could be recultivated.

Not so fortunate was Ching Hook's brother, Ching Kau, who lived three miles away on lower ground. Ching Kau lost two of his sons that day. The flood had washed away his home, forcing his family to flee for their lives. Ching Kau's eldest son was carrying his little brother on his back, and somehow they got separated from the rest of their family. Their bodies were found a few days later. (History would repeat itself in Anahola decades later. On a dark December night in 1991, another flood devastated the area, claiming four lives.)

Ching Hook and Kam Sing enjoyed life on Kaua'i, but they knew that better opportunities existed for their children elsewhere.

It was time to pack up and move the whole family to Honolulu. ❧

CHAPTER TWO
OLD
HONOLULU

OLD HONOLULU

When the four surviving siblings of Clarence Ching reminisce about their late brother, they point to the age difference between the family's older and younger children. Those remaining are Myrtle, Bernard and the twins, Gilbert and Herbert.

"We did not have a very close relationship with Clarence or the rest of the family," Herbert explained. "The other [siblings] were older, and they were always away at work. They had their own lives, their own problems, and the rest of us were just kids. After we finished high school, we went to the Mainland. And no sooner did we return than World War II broke out. There was a gas ration, and we only had ten gallons a month. Since we all lived in different areas, it was hard for us to see each other.

"Sad to say, the only times the whole family got together was when we had a wedding, a birthday party or a funeral."

Though the four do not recall much of their time in Anahola, they do remember why their father sold his mill and land and moved the family to Honolulu.

"He wanted us to get a better education," Bernard said. "He had the foresight to move the family to Oʻahu. He knew we would have better opportunities there."

Ching Hook, Kam Sing and their children moved to Honolulu in the early 1920s, settling into a two-bedroom home at the corner of Vineyard Boulevard and Liliha Street, where Times Supermarket is located today. After years of enjoying the lush surroundings of Anahola, living in the city was a major adjustment for the family.

Ching Hook found employment at the 27th Infantry Restaurant at Schofield Barracks, where his second son, Chow, worked as manager. Later, when Clarence and Clifford were old enough, they also helped Chow at the restaurant. Wrote Francis Lai Ching in *Ching Hook from Hung Mee*, "With the Chings working in the 27th Infantry Restaurant, the food there had the reputation among the servicemen of ranking as the very best in all of the Hawaiian Islands!"

Back then, of course, there were no freeways or highways. "When our father worked at the restaurant, transportation was so bad that he did not come home every day," recalls Herbert. "He usually stayed [at Schofield] and returned home on weekends. Even Clarence, when he started working out in the country as a bookkeeper, did not have a car. So he only came home about once a month."

Because life in the city was considerably more expensive, everyone did what they could to chip in. Kam Sing worked from home as a seamstress.

"I remember the boys had to walk to the factory to pick up the cloth for her to sew," says Myrtle. "In those days, the clothing was all pre-cut. It was a far walk for my brothers, but they would bring the cloth back for her. Our mother would sew everything, and then the boys would bring it back to the factory. That is how we got some extra income."

In time, Chow surprised his parents by buying them a house on Yamada Lane, just off Liliha Street and a short walk up from their previous dwelling. This house had four bedrooms and two bathrooms, providing the family with a much more comfortable living space.

Although the family was still poor, and would suffer through the Great Depression years, no one complained.

"We were never starving," Herbert recalled. "We always had food on the table. In fact, I used to tell my own kids, 'We ate better than you do!'"

Clarence attended Saint Louis School. The private Catholic Marianist school was founded in 1846 by the Catholic Missions under the direction of the Fathers of the Sacred Hearts of Jesus and Mary. Originally located in Windward Oʻahu, the school moved to a second location on River Street in downtown Honolulu.

By the time Clarence enrolled at Saint Louis, the school had just moved to its present location in Kaimukī.

Clarence might have been sickly and frail as a child, but he got stronger and more athletic as the years passed. In high school, he took up the extracurricular sport of boxing, and by the time he left school he was champion in the flyweight division.

"We knew he kept a punching bag in the garage, but we did not know about his boxing success," Herbert said. "That is how quiet and private he was. In those days, you had to create your own entertainment. Maybe boxing was the cheapest sport he could get into."

Clarence excelled in the classroom as well. He was twice elected President of his class and was a member of the school's Chinese Literary Improvement Association, an honorary society for students who posted a scholastic average of 85 percent or higher.

Clarence graduated from Saint Louis in 1932. Among his classmates was Kan Jung Luke, who would later become his close friend and business partner. Although he later took some college courses—"He went to night school, studying insurance and real estate," said his brother Bernard—Ching never earned a college degree.

Tragedy struck the Ching family in 1933, a year after Clarence graduated from high school. The Christmas season had always been a time of festive celebrations for the family. As Christmas drew closer that year, however, Kam Sing was experiencing severe headaches. The headaches became so intense that Ching Hook stayed home from work to tend to his beloved wife.

On the morning of Dec. 21, it seemed the worst had passed. "I feel just fine now," Kam Sing told her husband. Relieved, Ching Hook returned to work at the Schofield restaurant.

Later that day, on a rainy afternoon, Kam Sing began to feel ill again. The headaches returned, more intense than before. She asked her son Clifford to take her to a doctor. On the way over, however, she collapsed in the car, and Clifford drove back to the house in a state of panic.

Ching Hook and the oldest son, T.F., were immediately notified, and T.F. rushed over with a doctor. The headaches were unbearable now. Kam Sing looked to her physician and asked, "Is my head going to burst?"

When Ching Hook made it home, he ran inside and asked T.F., "How is your mother?"

"She is gone," was the reply.

Ching Hook was in disbelief. His precious Kam Sing, and the loving mother of his eleven children, was dead.

"His anguish and despair turned to frustrated anger as he left the bedroom and entered the living room," wrote Francis Lai Ching in *Ching Hook from Hung Mee*. "Seeing the festive looking Christmas tree, he snatched it up with all its ornaments and flung it out of the house before sinking into his chair in extreme dejection and distress. Outside, the rain continued to fall as if the heavens also joined in mourning with the Ching family who were heartbroken over Kam Sing's unexpected and sudden departure."

It was a devastating loss. Ching Hook and Kam Sing had made plans to return to China to spend their remaining years, and now Kam Sing was gone. As time passed, though, Ching Hook, who had saved enough money to purchase some land in his childhood village of Hung Mee, would return to his homeland, marry a middle-aged woman named Siu Shee and retire in the village.

In July 1947, Ching Hook, realizing he had done everything he could for his children, packed his bags and left Honolulu for good. On his journey back to China, he carried in his arms an urn carrying the remains of Kam Sing. He was returning her to her final resting place.

Ching Hook died on Sept. 30, 1952, at the age of 89.

• • •

Although Ching Hook and Kam Sing had passed on, they had accomplished their goal of providing the means to a better life for their children.

• T.F. worked at Dole's Hawaiian Pineapple Company for more than 20 years, serving as a department manager in freight and receiving. He was also part-owner of Boulevard Market.

• Chow managed and later owned the 27th Infantry Restaurant at Schofield with his brother-in-law, Chan Tam. When the restaurant's lease expired, he worked for the Army as a maintenance supervisor.

• Mae, the eldest daughter, took on the role of family matriarch. Everyone respected Mae, and she was affectionately given the nickname "The General" by her brothers and sisters.

• Mildred married and was a housewife.

• Clifford worked for the federal government as a budget analyst at Schofield Barracks until lung cancer claimed his life prematurely at 51.

• Myrtle married and worked at the Sheraton Moana Surfrider for fourteen years.

• Bernard attended Chicago Technical College to study refrigeration and air conditioning. This was made possible by financial support from Mae and her husband, Chan Tam. Bernard returned home and worked as a supervisor at Oahu Air Conditioning Company until he retired in 1985.

• Gilbert also studied refrigeration and air conditioning at Chicago Technical College, thanks in part to financial assistance from older brother Chow. Like Bernard, he worked for Oahu Air Conditioning Company.

• Herbert, with financial assistance from Clarence, studied engineering at Purdue University in Indiana. He put in 38 years of federal government service before retiring from Hickam Air Force Base in 1978.

• Leonard, the youngest sibling, spent 20 years in the Air Force before retiring and returning to Hawai'i, where he worked for Air Express International Corporation.

And what of the fifth child? What of Clarence T.C. Ching?

Clarence married Dorothy Sau Pung Tom, whom he met through a cousin. Dorothy, who graduated from McKinley High School, was warm, sincere and sweet— a remarkable woman whom everybody loved. One of ten children in her family, Dorothy was regarded as a mother figure among her siblings, including her younger sisters Alice Lum and Vivian Dang.

"She was like a mother to us. She took care of us," said Dang. "She was always thinking of others. She would go out of her way to help you. That is the kind of person she was."

Added Lum, "She was the best. She used to cook these big pots of soup, and everyone would come over and take home a pot. And the parties! She cooked enough food for these huge parties. Dot was so generous with her time. We can never forget someone like her."

In the late 1930s Dorothy's family opened a grocery store at Damon Tract, a residential and agricultural area next to the new John Rodgers Airport near Ke'ehi Lagoon. Clarence managed the store and ran the business.

Together, Clarence and Dorothy had three children: Lawrence, Wallace and Jocelyn. A fourth child, Lorraine, did not survive childbirth.

Clarence began dabbling in real estate work, but the enterprising businessman also kept his eyes open for any new opportunity that might come knocking.

Then he met a man named Sam Damon. &

DAMON TRACT

DAMON TRACT

In terms of his professional life, Clarence Ching's remarkable success story begins with the acquisition of Damon Tract, a 233-acre property nestled between Nimitz Highway and the old inter-island terminal at Honolulu International Airport. The acquisition would lead to successful developments in the area, which in turn led to subsequent land purchases and development deals, from Moanalua and Salt Lake to the Kukui Gardens affordable housing complex.

Honolulu's airport industrial area in the 21st century is a bustling maze encompassing auto dealerships, a small hotel, a drive-in, warehouses, home improvement retailers, a small shopping center and much more. By day, the area is typically so busy that finding an open parking space on the wide streets can be a challenge. It is an area thriving with business activity.

It was not always this way.

The story of how Damon Tract fell into the hands of Ching and his friend and business partner, K.J. Luke, can be traced as far back as the mid-nineteenth century. Centuries before, Hawai'i's ruling *ali'i* had created a system of land ownership called *ahupua'a*. The land was divided into sections that usually stretched from the mountain to the sea. These land divisions ranged in size from 100 to 100,000 acres.

In the nineteenth century, the ruling Kamehameha line claimed for itself the large *ahupua'a* of Moanalua on O'ahu. The 9,405-acre land division was eventually passed on to Bernice Pauahi Bishop, the great-granddaughter of Kamehameha I and the last descendant of the royal family line. When the kindhearted princess died in October 1884, her will deeded the property to Samuel Mills Damon, a business partner of her husband, Charles Reed Bishop. Part of the *ahupua'a*, which today stretches from Tripler Hospital down to the airport, included the area of Kaloaloa, better known as Damon Tract. Samuel Damon died in 1924, and the land was placed in a trust, the Damon Estate.

Until 1932, the estate rented sections of Damon Tract to sugar growers, who paid $7 per acre. That year, however, the rent jumped to $80 an acre.

Wrote Sanford Zalburg, of the *Honolulu Advertiser*: "Tenants were mostly small-wage earners who wanted land upon which to put up a modest home, plant some corn and tomatoes, raise some flowers. Maybe even have some chickens and ducks. There was no critical land shortage then, and some of these tenants sank all their money into improvements. They probably thought they would be there all their lives."

The residents of Damon Tract lived a simple and quiet life, with only occasional incidents interrupting the peace. One dramatic exception was the morning of Dec. 7, 1941, the day Japanese war planes attacked Pearl Harbor. A local newspaper reported a bomb crashing through the home of Damon Tract resident Thomas Fujimoto "while the family of three was eating breakfast. No one was injured, according to police. At 9:17 a.m., Damon Tract residents, according to a police report, were ordered to evacuate and the police said nearby residents were cooperating in helping them leave the area."

By the end of World War II, the real estate environment in Honolulu had changed. There was a boom in home building, and the big estates were planning housing subdivisions. Damon Estate was among those with ambitious plans, but as Zalburg's *Advertiser* article put it, "somehow it was left standing at the starting gate."

While rentals in 1950 were now going for $80 for a quarter of an acre, Damon Tract remained an area scattered with mostly substandard homes.

In February 1956, the Damon Estate took out an advertisement in the *Advertiser*, promoting "FACTS and TERMS for MODERNIZATION OF KALOALOA SUBDIVISION (Damon Tract)."

The ad read, in part: "For the last ten years the Trustees of the Estate of Samuel Mills Damon have worked toward the redevelopment of Kaloaloa, to make it a modern part of modern Honolulu. Zoning plans for a subdivision with city standards were submitted to the city in 1950 and approved. Recently revised lot plans were submitted to the city and now await approval.

"Costs for improvements alone will be over $3,000,000 and will include: Paved roads, sidewalks, curbs and gutters; Street lights; Sewers and storm drains; City water lines with standard pressure and volume; Fire hydrants.

"The redevelopment will be done in stages ... carefully and orderly. In fact, the entire development may take as long as four or five years, eliminating any possibility of mass dislocation.

"The Trustees of the Damon Estate are anxious to modernize the Damon Tract and make it an area of which the entire community will be proud. The new subdivision will have advantages as to location for military and civilian workers.

At the same time it will provide low-cost, modern homes with all city facilities and schooling and playgrounds for children which will contribute to making better citizens and a better Hawaii."

Under its plan for the new subdivision, Damon Tract would offer 55-year leases to tenants, with lots sized at a minimum of 5,000 square feet. In addition, low-cost financing would be made available through the Federal Housing Authority (FHA) for qualified buyers.

The estate dangled one other public relations carrot, insisting that existing tenants would be given the first opportunity to purchase the new homes. Existing homes that met FHA requirements, they added, would not need to be replaced. Homes below FHA standards that were improved to meet the federal requirements would also not necessarily be replaced.

The redevelopment, according to the Damon Estate, was simply a part of "the unstoppable march of progress."

Damon Tract residents were not impressed.

The Kaloaloa Community Association, a tightly knit group comprised of Damon Tract tenants, argued that the new subdivision would hike the price of land to an average of $1,100 an acre. In addition, they maintained, only one house in ten could qualify for FHA financing.

Further complicating matters was the Hawaiian Aeronautics Commission (HAC), which desired to take at least part of the Damon Tract land and use it to build a more modern, jet-age airport. The original 885-acre aviation facility, John Rodgers Airport, had been dedicated on March 21, 1927. It was named after Commander John Rodgers, who had been commanding officer of the Naval Air Station at Pearl Harbor from 1923 to 1925. He would later take part in the first-ever transpacific flight from San Francisco to Hawai'i. The airfield's name was officially changed to Honolulu Airport in 1947. Four years later, in April 1951, Hawai'i Gov. Ingram Stainback signed into law a bill that changed the name of the airport again, this time to Honolulu International Airport.

If the HAC planned to take the land in a few short years, the tenants reasoned, the residents would be sent packing. Why bother even talking about a new subdivision?

At least in the eyes of the Kaloaloa Community Association, that answer was obvious: The Damon Estate was simply trying to boost the value of the property to get more money from the HAC.

The book *Land and Power in Hawaii* supports that charge. "Here was a real squeeze," explained authors George Cooper and Gavan Daws. "The Damon trustees, who were having trouble getting rid of their tenants and thus upgrading the value of their property, thought that in a condemnation case the value of the land would be set, at least in part, according to the low lease rents being paid by tenants in ramshackle houses."

Damon Estate Trustee Herman V. Von Holt would later admit to the Honolulu media in 1958: "We faced a very decided risk of having the land condemned on the basis of how much income we were getting."

What followed was a bitter three-way battle, with the HAC seeking Damon Tract land, the Damon Estate looking to redevelop and the area residents fighting to maintain their way of life at Kaloaloa.

"At Damon Tract alongside Honolulu airport there is a mighty unhappy situation," wrote the *Honolulu Advertiser*'s Zalburg. "It's no fun for the 800 families— 3,271 persons—living there. It's no fun for the Damon Estate, which owns the land. Nor for the Hawaiian Aeronautics Commission which must take the land, apparently piece by piece, for a jet-age airport.

"Just when, the HAC, unfortunately, doesn't know."

As late as April 11, 1956, the Damon Estate seemed unwilling to blink. That day, a *Honolulu Star-Bulletin* article reported that the estate was not halting its plans for its $4.5-million residential improvement of Damon Tract. Samuel R. Damon, an estate Trustee and the grandson of Samuel Mills Damon, denounced HAC warnings that the advent of the jet age would make the proposed subdivision "untenable." According to the HAC, service hangars for jet aircraft would be located almost adjacent to the Damon land, subjecting residents to jet engine noise. Also, expansion plans for the airport would certainly require the absorption of at least a sizable portion of Damon Tract.

Sam Damon also blasted the HAC for publicizing its airport expansion plans "without first having the courtesy to contact the owners of the property."

One Damon Tract businessman with more than a passing interest in the situation was an ambitious developer named Clarence T.C. Ching.

By this time, Ching and Sam Damon were well acquainted. When Ching was tending the family store in Damon Tract, Damon would often drop in to purchase a few items—not the least of which were his favorite alcoholic beverages.

"Clarence had a liquor license," said his nephew Raymond Tam, "so besides canned goods, ice cream and soda pop, he also sold beer, wine and other liquor. When World War II came about, there was a big ration on alcohol. No longer could you just go to the store and say, 'I want a bottle of this and a bottle of that.' But Sam Damon loved his liquor, and my uncle made sure he got all the liquor he wanted. He would even use other people's ration coupons! So as you might expect, he and Clarence became very close friends."

Ching, K.J. Luke and Damon enjoyed regular golf outings at Waialae Country Club. Whenever the three men played, Damon would complain about the State's attempts to condemn Damon Tract to build a new airport. 'They're trying to steal the property from us!" he would say. The good-natured response from Ching and Luke was always the same: "If it is such a problem, you should sell Damon Tract to us."

Said Damon, "Go to hell!"

One day, after discussing the matter, Ching and Luke went to see Damon and presented him a sum of money.

"What is this for?" Damon asked, puzzled.

"Well, we are going to buy the property from you," said Luke.

"Who the hell said it was for sale?"

The two men smiled. "Well, the last time we talked, we asked you about selling it to us," they said, "and you never told us to go to hell!"

The hard truth, perhaps, was that Sam Damon had run out of options. The estate was in a tough situation with Damon Tract and was looking for a way out.

"This is what I think happened with Damon Tract," suggested Herbert Ching. "They had substandard homes. I know this because one of the guys that worked with me lived in the Damon Tract area. Sam Damon wanted to upgrade the homes there to meet FHA standards. They did a survey, and only 15 to 20 percent [of the homes] qualified as FHA approved. The rest had to be developed. But the tenants refused. They said, 'Why should we spend more money?' They were primarily low-income residents, so they could not afford to upgrade.

"They demonstrated at Bishop National Bank [later First Hawaiian Bank]. At the time, Damon was a Director of the bank. I remember this activist attorney representing the protestors, and they made a big scene. Of course, if you are the bank Director, you really cannot have people protesting like that. It was a mess. So I think one of the reasons Damon got rid of Damon Tract was to let somebody else worry about it."

Clarence T.C. Ching's parents, Ching Hook (left) and Kam Sing,
were married on Kaua'i in 1898.

Clarence stands fourth from the right, back row, in a family photo taken in the early 1930s.

Clarence was twice elected class President at Saint Louis School,
which had just moved to a new location in Kaimukī. Top: Senior class
photo in the school's 1932 yearbook.

Downtown Honolulu was a booming metropolis in the 1940s.
Opposite: Clarence's nephew Raymond (front) helps send off Clarence's
brothers Gilbert, Bernard and Herbert as they depart for the Mainland
aboard the *S.S. Lurline.*

A PROPHECY FULFILLED: THE STORY OF CLARENCE T.C. CHING

Opposite: Clarence and Dorothy's sons, Lawrence and Wallace.
Top: Lawrence, Clarence, Dorothy and Wallace, 1940s. Above: Wallace,
Dorothy, Jocelyn, Clarence and Lawrence, 1980s.

Clarence T.C. Ching was instrumental in developing former
Damon Estate lands into a premier mixed-use area of residential
subdivisions and light industrial parks.

On April 25, 1956—exactly two weeks after Sam Damon declared that the estate was proceeding with plans to redevelop Damon Tract—the *Honolulu Star-Bulletin*'s front-page headline announced: "Damon Tract Is Sold for $4.5 Million."

Clarence Ching and Kan Jung Luke had founded Loyalty Investment Company in the early 1950s, as well as a number of other companies with the "Loyalty" name. The company purchased Damon Tract, with Loyalty Development Company listed as the lessor.

"They made a very good team," said Warren Luke, K.J.'s son and the Chairman, CEO and President of Hawaii National Bank, which Ching and the elder Luke founded. "They both brought something to the table. They had known each other for a long time, and they just hit it off. Together, they did a lot of good things. They also did projects alone, and with other parties."

Not all of their ventures were successful. Early on, the two men bought into DuMont televisions and lost money. They invested in Nehi beverages and lost money. They tried their hand at some real estate—and lost money.

"They took risks," asserted Warren Luke. "Some were good, some were bad. In the beginning, it was not all cash flowing in. They had debts to pay. It was not easy. A lot of people think we were just handed everything, but we all came from humble beginnings. That's what happened here in Hawai'i. Immigrants came, they worked hard and they pulled together. That's the American way. You have hard times, but you work your way through them. That is what my father and Clarence did."

The terms of the Damon Tract sale included a $100,000 down payment. The remainder of the $4.5 million due was to be paid over a period of fifteen years.

The sale caused quite a stir in the local community. Many felt that the buyers had gotten an unbelievably generous deal. Others felt that they had overpaid. "A lot of people," said one observer, "felt that [Ching and Luke] were in over their heads."

The controversy over Damon Tract did not immediately vanish. Because the sale terms called for interest payments set at four percent a year (about $176,000 annually), Ching and Luke were forced to raise the rent for the Damon Tract tenants. On June 27, hundreds of protesters marched around the grounds of 'Iolani Palace, carrying signs emblazoned with "Save Our Homes!" and "Damon Tract Fights Back!"

When Ching and Luke announced that they had no immediate plans for the newly bought property, they were being truthful. Both men were prepared to hang on to Damon Tract as a long-term investment. They considered all possibilities, including enhancing and maintaining the area as a residential district. With the advent of the noisy jet age, however, Damon Tract would be better suited for an industrial park. In the end, both men knew that much of the property's future hinged on the redevelopment of the airport.

The partners recognized Damon Tract, like every other real estate deal or investment, was a risk, but they were in this for the long haul.

For nearly three decades, George Hong served as Ching's attorney and close confidant. Born and raised in Hawai'i, the Roosevelt graduate earned a degree in political science from the University of Hawai'i before being accepted to the prestigious Columbia Law School in New York. A lieutenant in the Army Reserve, he served fifteen months in Korea before returning to school and earning his law degree; then he relocated back to the Islands to start his law career.

"Clarence would actually have been satisfied to make a million dollars out of [his investment]," recalled Hong. "If someone had offered him a million dollars for it, he would have taken it."

But Ching and Luke would net a larger profit. Much larger.

Later that same year, on November 7, the partners sold a 25-acre parcel on the Ke'ehi Lagoon side of Lagoon Drive to Haris Associates for more than $1.6 million, or $1.50 per square foot. (Their purchase of Damon Tract had amounted to about 45 cents per square foot.) The following year, Haris Associates sold the same site for $2.35 a square foot to Century Investments.

Selling that small portion of the tract would help establish value for the remaining land should the HAC decide to purchase it. The resale only further heightened that value.

On March 28, 1957, the City Planning Commission finally took action, rezoning Damon Tract for airport and industrial use. The Territorial government condemned 67 acres of the tract, saying that land was needed to expand Honolulu International Airport.

Four months later, on July 28, the official announcement was made: Sixty-seven acres were sold to the HAC for a compromise price of $4.95 million, or $1.68 per square foot. Of the 233 acres the partners purchased in 1956, they had sold 92 for a $2.1 million profit and still had 141 left.

More than four decades later, the *Honolulu Star-Bulletin* would call Ching and Luke's purchase of Damon Tract "one of the greatest coups in the history of Hawai'i land sales."

In an August 11, 1958, interview with Sanford Zalburg of the *Star-Bulletin*, Luke insisted that he was not necessarily happy with selling part of Damon Tract to the HAC.

"I'd very much like to have the land back," he told Zalburg. "I have an offer right here in my safe for $3.50 a square foot for some of this land. Just this morning, a man called me and asked: 'You sure you don't want to sell part of the land?' The need for industrial property is terrific. Not a day goes by that people don't call me and ask me about it. And these are genuine offers—backed by certified checks."

He had a point. The advantages of building an industrial park in the area were obvious. The area was close to the harbor and airport and just minutes away from the heart of town.

Ching and Luke would have the remaining 141 acres of Damon Tract to subdivide into industrial lots. Together, they developed the land and ushered in a new era for that part of Honolulu.

Summarized Cooper and Daws in *Land and Power in Hawaii*: "These transactions told the old money of Hawai'i that local-Asian businessmen were growing up in their midst with certain capabilities and with a drive that men like the trustees of the great estates simply had to acknowledge. If the Damon trustees did not want the headaches and preferred to sell, Ching and Luke were ready to buy, with the expectation that hard work, intelligence, political connections, and the likelihood of substantial profits would take care of the headaches."

Damon Tract established Ching and Luke as major players in Hawai'i's real estate and development community.

And they were just getting started. ❧

GROWING WITH THE COMMUNITY

GROWING WITH THE COMMUNITY

While Damon Tract had helped put Clarence Ching on the map as a Hawai'i developer, it certainly was not his first venture. In the early 1950s, as the head of City Realty, he oversaw the development of several small subdivisions, including three in Nu'uanu, two near the University of Hawai'i and one in Kāne'ohe. The success he and K.J. Luke had in purchasing Damon Tract, however, emboldened him to seek bigger, more ambitious projects. He saw needs in the local community that he wanted to help fill. All he needed, he felt, was the right vehicle.

Enter, once again, Sam Damon.

No one is sure of the exact date, but sometime early in January 1957, the two friends happened to be on the same flight from Honolulu to San Francisco. They sat next to each other and began making small talk. Then, seemingly out of the blue, Damon leaned over to Ching and asked, "Do you want to buy the entire *ahupua'a* of Moanalua?"

According to people familiar with the story, Ching hesitated for just a moment. "Sure," he replied. "How much?"

Damon looked straight at him. "Nine million dollars."

Ching laughed and shook his head in disbelief. "You know I do not have that kind of money," he countered.

Damon, however, was in a mood to deal. "Clarence," he said, "I trust you. You just pay me as you develop."

With a simple handshake, the deal was struck. And now not only did Ching have the vehicle he wanted; he was sitting in the driver's seat.

Officially, the deal transferred 1,074 acres to a partnership, with Ching serving as the principle organizer. The land included Salt Lake and Moanalua's two pristine valleys.

Sam Damon never lived to see what his friend would do with Moanalua. He died of a heart attack on August 29, 1957, while on a flight bound for Seattle.

By this time, Ching had a desire to test the waters of Hawai'i's low-cost housing market. The Federal Housing Authority, recognizing the need for multi-family housing, was beginning to provide low-cost financing programs to attract interested developers. As the June 1970 edition of *Hawaii Business* magazine later reported, however, "few developers have had the patience or the organizational capability to work their way through the red tape involved in government-assisted housing programs."

One who was willing to try was Ching. He approached the FHA about building an apartment complex in Moanalua—the Moanalua Hillside Apartments—and then patiently snipped his way through every piece of government red tape that blocked his path.

A November 1, 1957, *Honolulu Advertiser* story reported that the City Planning Commission had approved plans for a 25,000-resident, multimillion-dollar housing development in Moanalua. The project would be built by International Development Company (of which Ching was a partner) on land bought from the Damon Estate.

More details of the venture were revealed the next day, when the *Advertiser* reported that Hawaiian Dredging & Construction Company was already clearing land for a "rush increment" of 200 home sites on land bordering Fort Shafter. Ching explained that the next increment would likely border Salt Lake, just *makai* of Moanalua Highway. Upon completion, he said, the area would contain a marina, restaurants and a private park—in addition to 3,500 planned home sites.

Noted the *Advertiser*: "As for the lake itself, [Ching] said studies are still being made to determine its boundaries and depth. It will be impossible to suck out much of the mud covering the lake's bottom, increasing the present eleven-foot depth another five or six feet."

The lake would later prove to be the center of a major controversy. At the time, however, Ching was more concerned about negotiating with the government to make Moanalua Hillside a reality.

"It was a period of interminable wrangling, as business, bound by the dictates of profit, met head on with the rules and regulations of government," *Hawaii Business* reported. "FHA spelled out standards which had to be met in virtually every phase of the project, but the developer had to incorporate these into an economically viable form. And as a limited distribution mortgagor, the developer was held to a six percent return on his investment."

"It was a real can of worms," admitted Ching in the article. "And not only was it new to us, it was essentially new to the FHA people, too. The program had been in effect only a few years, and we were the first large project in Hawaii to use it. FHA sent specialists out from Washington, and we made a number of trips back there to try to figure out ways to get together."

In the end, Moanalua Hillside Apartments was deemed a success, and this first venture into low-cost housing development would eventually help Ching land a similar project in downtown Honolulu. This was Kukui Gardens, the development that Ching's closest associates would call "his pride and joy."

Reported *Hawaii Business*: "Hawaii was already in the throes of the tract development fever [in 1957], and for a time Ching considered going that route with some of his property. However, that would have meant tying up a lot of money for a long time, and Ching likes the kind of deal where his money does not long remain idle, even if it means taking a smaller piece of the pie.

"Moreover, despite the skepticism of some of his collaborators, he was convinced that there was a strong market for improved house sites among individual buyers who didn't want tract housing. The issue was finally settled when his first offering, 170 fee simple house lots adjoining Fort Shafter, went on the market. They were sold out in forty-eight hours.

"Eventually another 200 lots were offered and snapped up in the same project, which became known as Moanalua Gardens. Although the land was fee simple, selling for about $10,000 to $13,000, the agreement of sale spelled out certain design and construction requirements which assured esthetic harmony in the development—a procedure which was to be followed in later Ching developments around Salt Lake."

• • •

Next on Clarence Ching's agenda, the *Hawaii Business* article noted, was a major development at Salt Lake. A December 2, 1958, *Honolulu Star-Bulletin* headline previewed a 4,000-home subdivision in the area: "Developers See Salt Lake As a Beach Resort Area."

"Standing at the tip of a rocky finger that jabs into Salt Lake, it's hard to believe that you're only a five-minute drive from Honolulu's bustle," the accompanying story began. "There's no noise there, except the whoosh of a stiff breeze that kicks up waves on the 250-acre lake. The only life visible is at a weather-stained cottage and cluster of outbuildings directly across from the point.

"Perhaps you couldn't see this as a booming resort area, with white sand beaches, fashionable hotels and apartment houses and facilities for water skiing, boating and the like.

"But that's the vision held by a group of men who call themselves the International Development Company (IDC)."

IDC was set up by Loyalty Enterprises and its officials, specifically Ching and K.J. Luke, to serve as developer of the subdivision. The timetable for the project's completion was about ten years, and by then, Ching estimated, the subdivision should be worth at least $100 million. People were heralding it as the biggest fee simple project in the Territory of Hawai'i.

Sometimes, however, even the best plans need to be reshaped.

Flash forward to 1964. By this time, Ching had concluded that maintaining the lake was simply too cost-prohibitive. Furthermore, the water quality was poor and still deteriorating due to past misuse. Since the 1950s, the military had been dumping waste into the lake from its housing facilities in nearby Āliamanu Crater. Thus, any further thoughts of using it for boating, waterskiing or swimming were put to rest.

"This is where Clarence really displayed his vision," recalled George Hong, who served as Ching's attorney and advisor. "Since the lake was not really usable, I asked him what he was going to do with it. And he told me, 'I am going to fill the lake and make a golf course out of it.' He possessed such a great mind and vision."

Added an observer who knew Ching and Luke well: "They kind of did it backwards, when you think about it. Normally, you would build a golf course, then sell homes around it. You would tell prospective homebuyers, 'Look, here is a nice golf course that will be close to your house.' But what they did was sell the home lots first, and then built the golf course."

The name of the subdivision was Lakeside, and plans called for 1,100 residential lots and 300 apartment building lots constructed over a six-year period. The proposed golf course would be a challenging eighteen-hole layout, plus a country club, all sitting on the site of the lake.

On July 18, 1965, more than 700 business, civic and government leaders attended a ceremonial *lū'au* at the Damon residence in Salt Lake to bless the $20-million development. The program included a three-part ceremony conducted by David Bray, Sr., one of Hawai'i's best-known *kahuna*. First, on the future site of a proposed elementary school, Bray lit a sacrificial fire using wood from *kiawe* trees that had grown on the project site. Next, Ching and Pat Carscadden, project manager for general contractor

Hawaiian Dredging & Construction Company, boated with Bray to the middle of the lake. As the *Honolulu Advertiser* described it: "Bray blessed a large stone taken from the area and poured bottles of brandy and gin over a mullet, *kumu*, egg and taro. They were placed in a container, tied to the stone, and dropped over the side where they plunged to the bottom of the lake to appease the Hawaiian gods dwelling there."

The third part of the blessing took place at the far side of the lake, where a ceremonial pig was cooked in a traditional *imu*. "Bray offered the pig, along with the remainder of his eggs, taro, fish and liquor, to the gods in a ceremony that was considered the most important part of the ritual," reported the *Advertiser*.

The IDC's plan to fill nearly 200 acres of the lake to build a golf course, however, ran into a roadblock. Preservationists from organizations such as the Audubon Society, Outdoor Circle, Garden Club and League of Women Voters were against filling the lake. "Salt Lake is the only natural lake in Hawai'i," they insisted, "and should be protected, not turned into a golf course." Salt Lake, they pointed out, was formed centuries ago from an extinct volcanic crater. Early Hawaiians called the body of water *aliapa'akai*, or "salt-encrusted."

Supporters of the golf course argued that Salt Lake was an artificial lake—and had been so for the past five decades. A public hearing was set for August 26, 1966, to settle the dispute.

In *Land and Power in Hawaii*, George Cooper and Gavan Daws provided insight into the history of Salt Lake: "At about the end of the [nineteenth] century [Samuel Mills] Damon leased land around the lake to a sugar plantation," they wrote. "Runoff from the cane fields silted up the lake, by some later accounts plugging the salt spring. In any event, in 1910 the plantation had an artesian well dug nearby that supplied a large amount of fresh water. The water was dumped into the lake to provide a steady source for irrigation. For whatever reason, the lake no longer produced salt."

Henry Damon, grandson of Samuel Mills Damon, appeared at the hearing to set the record straight about the lake's history. "The lake," he insisted, "has existed in its present state only since 1910."

Damon, whose home looked down on the lake, expressed his support for the construction of the golf course.

"It's much better to make use of the area as a golf course, and not have the problem of trying to make a very muddy area clean," he maintained.

By the time the meeting adjourned, members of the State Department of Land

and Natural Resources recommended that Salt Lake be converted into the golf development. Two weeks later, the Land Board followed up on the recommendation and officially gave International Development Company the go-ahead. Ching and his partners had emerged victorious in a key battle. Island historians consider this controversy one of the biggest environmental-developmental battles in modern Hawai'i.

Ironically, although Ching fought hard to get the lake filled to build his golf course, he was not there to put the finishing touches on the course when it was completed. In 1973, he sold the Salt Lake acreage for $4.5 million to Stan Himeno, President of Y&H Corporation.

After further delays and false starts, the course finally made its debut in March 1977. Hawai'i residents know it today as the Honolulu Country Club.

• • •

Clarence Ching had long wanted to start his own bank. Before the fall of 1960, the two major banks in the state—Bank of Hawai'i and First Hawaiian Bank (then Bishop National Bank)—received 80 percent of the deposits. The smaller banks, generally the ones owned by local Asian businessmen, seemingly picked up the scraps.

When the Democrats had taken political control of Hawai'i in the early 1950s, however, the climate had changed. "As with so many other areas of life, the coming to power of the Democrats overturned that old arrangement," Cooper and Daws wrote in *Land and Power in Hawaii*. "This meant that the smaller man, the new man, the man who might not have been *haole*, the man who might not have gotten good treatment when he went to one of the old banks for a loan, now had a chance to get ahead."

"Clarence and K.J. felt there was a need for a bank," said one observer. "In those days, a lot of Asians were not treated all that well by the big financial institutions."

With the help of his friend, U.S. Congressional Delegate and future Hawai'i Governor John A. Burns, the new bank was able to get its required federal charter in December 1959. Approximately 160,000 shares of common stock were made available, and an eager public gobbled them up immediately, helping the bank launch with $2.8 million right off the bat.

Originally, the bank was to be called the National Bank of Honolulu, but the name was soon changed to Hawaii National Bank, to better reflect the loftier ambitions of the bank's Directors.

George Hong recalled that initially Luke was not even in favor of starting the bank. "I remember Clarence and K.J. talking about it," Hong said. "K.J. was not for it. But when he saw that Clarence was going ahead with it, he went along, too."

As usual, Luke served as the public face of the bank, while Ching took his preferred place behind the scenes. Officially, Ching was the bank's Vice President and a Director, while Luke served as its Board Chairman and President.

With the ceremonial cutting of a *maile* lei and an explosion of firecrackers, Hawaii National Bank opened its doors to the public for the first time on September 19, 1960. Located at the corner of North King and Smith Streets in downtown Honolulu, the bank welcomed hundreds of visitors, who were entertained by musical bands representing six different cultures. By the end of that first day, the bank had collected some $6.25 million—a new record for opening-day deposits.

One highlight during the bank's first week of business was its "lucky coins" promotion. Each visitor received a special coin inscribed with a "lucky number." Drawings were held, and the winners were awarded savings accounts ranging from $10 to $250.

According to *American Banker* magazine, Hawaii National Bank was the largest of the 134 banks to open for business in the United States during that year.

By 1967, the bank had already opened six new branches, in the Airport Industrial Park, Hawai'i Kai, Makiki, Waikīkī, Kailua and Kaimukī. An advertisement in the October 2, 1967, edition of the *Honolulu Star-Bulletin* touted, "Hawaii National Bank's openings are always exciting events with tens of thousands of firecrackers set off, prize contests, the traditional cutting of the *maile* lei and food novelties. At the Kailua branch opening, even the fortune cookies responded to the occasion: "The next hand you shake will be that of a warm-hearted banker." "Money is the root of all interest." "Happiness is a balanced check book." "Save now, play later."

The ad, which also trumpeted the bank's seventh anniversary, further stated: "All services are slanted toward the convenience of the customer, and friendly personalized interest in each individual's problems. Their slogan, 'Headquarters of the Warm-Hearted Bankers,' is a serious statement of their concept of good banking practices, and no customer finds his financial concerns, however small, received with less than maximum care and attention."

At the time, bank robberies in Hawai'i were a rarity. An August edition of the *Honolulu Advertiser* reported that there had been only six bank robberies in the state since 1934—and "nearly all of them were bungled."

One of the six had occurred earlier in the year, on May 16. That day, a 24-year-old escaped convict robbed Hawaii National Bank's Waikīkī branch. Just an hour later, police arrested the culprit when they spotted him at Honolulu International Airport carrying a paper sack containing $5,000.

But nothing would top the events of robbery attempt number seven, which occurred at the same Waikīkī branch of Hawaii National Bank. On August 25, a man walked into the branch and passed a note to the bank teller behind the window—the same window the previous robber had walked up to just three months earlier.

The note read, "Please hand me $3,000 in 20s and 50s. No fooling around. I have a gun."

This teller, however, was having none of it. Instead, 21-year-old Judy Youngman simply looked at the note, closed her cash drawer and walked out of the cage. Said assistant cashier Jess Ramos to a reporter, "She just came up and handed me the note, calm as can be."

The befuddled robber turned around, ran out the door and disappeared down Kalākaua Avenue.

A large photo of a smiling Youngman talking with a police detective appeared in the next day's *Honolulu Advertiser.* "A nervy bank teller turned her back on a would-be robber...." the story began.

In 1978, Clarence Ching parted company with Hawaii National Bank. He and K.J. Luke had been buying up stock in Liberty Bank, and Ching joined Liberty Bank as a Director. His son, Lawrence, was President of the bank by then. Lawrence headed Liberty Bank from 1975 to 1993, when it was purchased by Bank of America Hawai'i. Lawrence was only 39 when he became the bank's President, making him the youngest-ever President of a Hawai'i bank.

• • •

No one could ever accuse Clarence Ching of forgetting his roots. The son of Chinese immigrants was President of the Sun Yat-sen School, President of the Ching Clan Society and President of the Chinese Chamber of Commerce. But perhaps the best evidence of his commitment to the Chinese people was his involvement in the construction of the Chinese Cultural Plaza in downtown Honolulu.

Chinatown's story is one of inspiration and tragedy. By 1884, nearly 100 years after the first Chinese immigrants arrived in Hawai'i from southern China, the Chinese population in Honolulu had reached 5,000. Although plantation work was on the decline, the Chinese were as enterprising as they were hardworking, and many of them opened their own shops and businesses on O'ahu. About 75 percent of the local Chinese were concentrated in a 25-acre area downtown.

In 1886, a fire destroyed most of Chinatown, claiming the residences of 7,000 Chinese and 350 native Hawaiians. Even larger fires burned through Chinatown in 1900, but this time the fires were deliberately set by the Board of Health in an effort to wipe out the bubonic plague that had been spreading in the area.

In the ensuing years, Chinatown—and Honolulu's Chinese—endured. But Clarence Ching decided that something was missing.

"He realized that there was a need for a place where the Chinese could meet and convene," said his nephew Raymond Tam.

The headline screamed across the front page of the October 26, 1964, edition of the *Honolulu Advertiser*: "Pacific Culture, Trade Complex Planned for Chinatown."

"The first step has been taken toward development of a multimillion-dollar Pacific area cultural center and trade mart complex covering a two-block portion of the Kukui Redevelopment Area in downtown Honolulu," reported Emil A. Schneider, the newspaper's business editor. "The project is being sponsored by five of the leading societies of the Chinese community here."

Ching, 52 years old at the time, was designated the Chairman of Cultural Plaza Inc., which included the Sun Yat-sen School, the Lung Doo Society, the Chee Tung Society, the Kuo Min Tang Society and the Leong Jung Society. The complex was to be bordered by Beretania and Kukui Streets, and by Maunakea and River Streets.

The vision for the complex—projected to cost from $8 to $12 million—called for retail and meeting facilities for cultural groups of Chinese Americans and others of Asian ancestry, language and art schools, restaurants and entertainment venues, and a trade mart with product displays, offices, auditorium facilities and more.

"We must, at all costs, develop this commercial area of Kukui," Ching told the *Advertiser*. "We must relocate the societies, people and business firms in old Chinatown; renew Chinatown in accordance with an orderly, planned program that will still preserve the architectural design and the flavor of Chinatown; accommodate our Pacific area neighbors through the Trade Mart; and achieve our destiny, which is to become the economic bridgehead between East and West."

With that proclamation, the seed for the Chinese Cultural Plaza was planted.

"The local Chinese wanted to name the whole thing after him, but he refused," noted Ray Tam. "He told them, 'This is not for me. This is for you, the Chinese people.'"

Certainly, the project was ambitious, almost grandiose in its vision. Although the original timetable for the complex's completion was three years, such a major undertaking was bound to experience delays—and so it did.

It took two years just for the design plan to be approved by the Honolulu Redevelopment Agency (HRA). The design concept, masterminded by John Carl Warnecke & Associates for Cultural Plaza Inc., called for 1,000 apartment units, 294,000 square feet of commercial space, 226,000 square feet for cultural activities, enough street parking for 2,000 cars and approximately seven acres of open space.

Traffic congestion in the area was one primary concern. "The Warnecke firm has prepared studies which offer an alternate solution to the traffic problem," reported the *Honolulu Advertiser* on July 12, 1966. "This involves opening River Street to traffic, which could then replace Maunakea Street as the makai-mauka connector. River Street would become a tree-lined quay with boating activities on Nuuanu Stream on one side and open plazas, outdoor restaurants and access to the Center on the other."

Nearly four years later, however, the planned construction of the plaza was still stuck at the starting gate. In January 1970, the Honolulu Chinese Jaycees sponsored a Cultural Plaza Expo to familiarize the public with the project. The event promised rides, games, food and entertainment, but like the plaza itself, not everything went according to plan.

"At about 8 p.m., there was a power failure and most of the lights and all of the rides were off for about a half hour," wrote Lois Taylor in the *Honolulu Star-Bulletin*. "The lion did his thing by dancing around and shaking his gorgeous sequined head and stomping his basketball shoes, but the small children who wanted to ride the electric boats or the merry-go-round were out of luck."

The brief power failure seemed to capture perfectly the stop-and-go nature of the plaza project: full of promise and ambition, but marred by frequent stalls and false starts. Among the reasons for the delays were financing problems, logistical dilemmas and bickering among the Chinese societies involved in the project.

At long last, ground was broken for the plaza's construction on December 6, 1972. The next day, the *Honolulu Advertiser* noted, "Only hours before the 3 p.m. groundbreaking ceremony, the developers finally secured their interim financing from Liberty Bank and the Irving Trust Company of New York. That clinched the deal on a project that has been more talk than action for the past ten years."

In March 1974, Ching announced that, barring further delays, the $11-million cultural plaza would open that September. Naturally, there were delays. The plaza finally made its debut in January of 1975, with a public celebration attended by several hundred people. Firecrackers were set off to drive out evil spirits. A ferocious dancing lion thrilled young and old alike. The festive evening included everything from kung fu demonstrations to free refreshments.

"It's something unique that you don't see anywhere else in America where Chinese groups get together and form a *hui* (an association or group)," one official pointed out to a *Honolulu Star-Bulletin* reporter. "It's hard to get six Chinese organizations together as one *hui*. Everybody has their own mind so it's very hard."

The Chinese Cultural Plaza is still standing at its original location today.

"Clarence said that the plaza project was strictly for the societies, not for him," said Hong. "He just wanted to help. He was loyal to his Chinese roots, and he always did everything he could to help the Chinese in Hawai'i." ❧

CHAPTER FIVE
A QUIET
LEADER

A QUIET LEADER

Clarence Ching was never the type of man to draw attention to himself. As a result, media coverage providing insights on Ching the businessman and community leader was almost nonexistent. The most noteworthy profile on Ching, in fact, was a lengthy feature in the June 1970 issue of *Hawaii Business* magazine—and even that piece focused primarily on the projects rather than the man himself. In terms of his personality and character, he was described only as "taciturn but action-minded."

"I would not necessarily say he was like [former Hawai'i Governor] George Ariyoshi—you know, 'Quiet and Effective'—but he was close," said Honolulu attorney Peter Ng. "There was nothing flashy about him. He just did his job. He knew what he wanted done, and he got it done. When he said something, people listened."

A partner in Ng & Niebling, LLC, Ng has practiced law for more than 40 years, specializing in estate planning, wills and trusts, probate and guardianships. He worked with Ching as a Board member for the Saint Louis-Chaminade Education Center and on the Kukui Gardens Corporation Board.

"He was reserved, but he carried a punch," Ng recalled. "He was always respected. People listened to him because of his knowledge and his ability to do things positively and profitably in business."

The Kukui Gardens Corporation Board meetings run by Ching were painstakingly efficient. "He ran every meeting precisely," Ng recounted. "There was no unwanted or prolonged discussion on any matter. He always had an agenda ready, and he stuck to it. He would say, 'Okay, all in favor…?' And then he would ask, 'All who are contrary-minded…?' He was very direct and abrupt at the Kukui Gardens meetings. There was no wasted talk or energy."

As Ching's attorney and confidant, George Hong worked closely with the developer for nearly a quarter-century. Hong marveled at the way Ching processed information.

"I used to meet with Clarence every morning, and we would discuss things," Hong recalled. "Actually, I did all the talking, and he hardly talked at all. He would just sit behind his desk, listening. And then, later on, he would tell me what he wanted. It would come out of his mouth, like *bang, bang, bang….*"

Added Carol Hong, George's daughter: "I worked for my father, and I remember sitting in meetings with him and Mr. Ching. Mr. Ching was extraordinarily good with numbers. My father would try to add up figures, and Mr. Ching would just rattle off the numbers from his head."

Dorothy Tam Ching worked for her uncle for nearly 20 years, first as an office clerk and then as his secretary. The office environment was always casual and friendly.

"It was very pleasant. Mr. Ching never grumbled or yelled at anyone," she observed. "He was a very easygoing gentleman to work for. He made sure that he knew everybody's name. He was not the type of boss who just sat in his office. He liked to walk around and speak to his employees. Everyone could call him by his first name."

Dorothy, whose mother, Mae, was Clarence's oldest sister, had never imagined herself as her uncle's secretary. After graduating from Roosevelt High School, she attended the Colorado State College of Education at Greeley (now the University of Northern Colorado). When she applied for a position at Loyalty Enterprises in downtown Honolulu, she was offered a clerical job. When his secretary left the firm a few years later, Ching asked his niece to take her job.

Ching took good care of his employees. "He gave us as many benefits as possible," said Dorothy. "We had free medical and a full month's salary as a Christmas bonus. He was just a great man to work for."

Another close associate of Clarence Ching was Gene Tiwanak. The two men became acquainted in 1973 after Tiwanak joined St. Francis Medical Center to head the hospital's fund development committee and lay advisory panel. The panel included business and community luminaries such as Ching, Maurice J. Sullivan, Frank Hata and Nancy Walker.

"With Clarence and Sully on the Board, everybody said that I had the easiest job in the world," Tiwanak recalled. "And in a way, they were right. We were successful because of those guys."

At the time, the hospital fell under the leadership of Sister Maureen Keleher, who served as CEO from 1953 to 1988. Under her direction, St. Francis Medical Center became a leader in organ transplants. (The first heart transplant in Hawai'i was performed at St. Francis.) In the late 1970s, she pioneered the concept of hospice care in Hawai'i, introducing Hawai'i's first hospice program and providing terminally ill patients with attentive care outside of the hospital.

"In our Board meetings, Sister Maureen would ask, 'Mr. Ching, what do you think?'" Tiwanak said. "And his answer would always be short. There was no dissertation! And then after the meeting he would call me and say, 'What does Sister want?' That is how he was. His business style was very quiet and understated. These days, you see everybody trying to take a front position. That was never Clarence."

Clarence Ching's connections with Hawai'i's top political players were well known. For example, he was a close confidant of John A. Burns, who served three terms as the state's Governor, from 1962 until 1974. Like Ching, Burns was an alumnus of Saint Louis School. He later served as Captain of the Honolulu Police Department and then, in 1948, gained political clout as Chair of the Democratic County Committee. Burns served as a Territorial Delegate to the U.S. Congress from 1957 to 1959 and was a key player in helping Hawai'i achieve statehood.

As recounted in *Land and Power in Hawaii*, Ching approached Burns for help in 1959, when Burns was a Delegate. Ching had applied for a federal charter for what would become Hawaii National Bank and felt that the Territory's two large banks were unfairly trying to stonewall the application. Burns was a close friend of U.S. Senate Majority Leader and future U.S. President Lyndon B. Johnson, and he persuaded Johnson to use his influence to get the federal charter approved.

Later that year, after his failed attempt to become Hawai'i's first Governor, Burns was low on funds. Ching offered him some financial assistance. According to *Land and Power*, Burns declined the gift, telling Ching, "You keep that money and give Merchant Street hell."

Ching later served as Burns' principal fundraiser throughout the 1960s, helping his friend attain the governorship. He was also close with Burns' Lieutenant Governor, George Ariyoshi, who would himself serve three terms at Washington Place (Ariyoshi was the first American of Asian descent to be elected as Governor of a U.S. state), as well as Neal Blaisdell, who served as Honolulu's Mayor from 1955 to 1969. Before entering politics, Blaisdell was a football coach at Saint Louis School, where he coached future all-American Herman Wedemeyer.

According to Dorothy Ching, Clarence's niece and secretary, her uncle's support for Governor Burns had little to do with gaining political favor. "He really believed in Governor Burns," she said.

Nevertheless, Ching was never too proud to ask for help when he needed it.

"One of the reasons that Clarence was so successful was that he surrounded himself with talented people," explained Herbert Ching. "If he wanted financial advice, he could go to a certain person. If he wanted a subdivision plan, he could go to another."

Ching had a great deal of respect for Maurice Sullivan, who came to the U.S. from Ireland at the age of seventeen and, in 1948, co-founded Foodland Supermarkets. Sullivan and his partner See Goo Lau opened the first Foodland at the Market City Shopping Center, which was owned by Hiram Fong.

"I usually sat between Clarence and Maurice, who I considered my two most powerful Board members," recalled Tiwanak of his St. Francis Board meetings. "Clarence would come in and sit down, and after a while it looked like he had fallen asleep! He would sit there with his eyes closed while presentations were being made. And then all of a sudden, no matter what problem we were discussing, he would lean over to me and say, 'Tell the Sister no worry. Go see the Governor.' And then he would put his head down again. It was amazing. And after the meeting was over, he would tell me again: 'Call Dorothy [his secretary]. Tell her to set up an appointment for you to see George [Ariyoshi]. Tell him what the Sister wants.'"

George Hong praised Ching's leadership ability. "The one thing I most remember about Clarence was that he always kept his word," he said. "If he said something, you could rely on it. And that is sometimes rare in the business he was in."

Ching played an instrumental role in helping St. Francis open a hospital in 'Ewa in 1990. It remains the only major health care facility in West O'ahu. In the early 1980s, St. Francis management was seeking to expand services on O'ahu. At the same time, Pearlridge Hospital (where Kapi'olani Medical Center at Pali Momi stands today) was about to cease operations. St. Francis sought to claim the hospital's license, along with several other medical facilities.

The St. Francis Board looked to the Pearlridge site to fulfill its expansion plans. The relatively small size of the area (three acres), however, was not conducive to any future expansion.

Still, the advisory Board was split, with half of the members wanting to build on the Pearlridge Hospital site.

Ching favored a location that was further west. "The Leeward area is going to grow," he advised Sister Maureen and the rest of the Board. "You have to move out, go beyond Pearlridge. Go into the Leeward area."

Sullivan also preferred a Leeward location. He had a Foodland market in Pearl

City and was himself eying the ʻEwa Beach area for another store site.

Dissent to Ching's recommendation was understandable; most of the Leeward area was still blanketed with sugar cane fields. Sister Maureen, however, decided to go with Ching's recommendation. She directed Tiwanak to speak to the other advisory panel members and convince them that building a hospital in West Oʻahu was the best possible option. "We will not have a vote until you have done this," she added.

Recalled Tiwanak, "Then Clarence did something that really pulled everybody together. Also on the Board at the time was City Councilman George Akahane, who was very close to Clarence. George knew the [Leeward] area and, at Clarence's urging, gave the Board more confidence in making the decision to head west."

The vote was unanimous, paving the way for St. Francis Medical Center-West (now Hawaii Medical Center West).

"If it were not for Clarence's foresight and assistance," Tiwanak said, "the Leeward area would not have gotten the medical center it has today. And that was needed to really begin development of that area. It became a magnet for people who could say, 'It is okay to move there; we will not be too far from a hospital.'"

Just how much did Clarence Ching benefit the St. Francis Medical Center? In 1973, the hospital's operating budget was in the neighborhood of $16 million. By 1985, the year of Ching's death, the estimated operating budget was more than $200 million.

When Ching died in 1985, his eldest son, Lawrence, took his place on the St. Francis advisory panel.

Another facet of Clarence Ching the businessman was his continued allegiance to his family. Even after earning wealth and acclaim for his professional successes, Ching always consulted with his oldest sister, Mae, before announcing any major business move.

"My mother [Mae] was considered the matriarch of the family after their mother died," said Raymond Tam. "All her brothers and sisters called her 'The General.' Clarence always called her before going forward on a big decision. I do not think he called her to seek her advice or input. He did not need that from her. He already knew what he wanted to do. I think he called her out of respect. He wanted to receive her blessing."

Clarence's generosity was always appreciated by his family. "When I lived in Kapahulu, we did not have much money to buy things," recalled Clarence's sister, Myrtle. "Every once in a while, he used to bring his daughter's clothes and toys for our kids. He always thought about us. That is the kind of man he was."

At home, Ching maintained a simple diet. In the morning, the standard fare was a soft-boiled egg, half a papaya served at room temperature and toast. At night, before he went to bed, he would enjoy a glass of warm milk to help him sleep.

Major General Stephen Tom, of the U.S. Army Reserve, recalls his uncle Clarence as a generous and caring man.

"He never really talked about himself, but he was always interested in what you were doing," said Tom, who is Chief of Staff of the United States Pacific Command. "I remember going up to their house in the 1960s. They always had the newest televisions, the newest cars and the most modern appliances. I was really attracted to that. I loved seeing what was there. They would have these Sunday night dinners for the family, and they were really fun. But even then, he would mostly stay in the background."

Tom recalls a time he and his cousins were looking for summer jobs.

"This was 1969, right in the middle of the development of Kukui Gardens, so we thought, 'Let us go into construction,'" said Tom. "Some cousins were doing painting, and others would install faucets or bathtubs. But when I went to talk to him, I guess he had a different plan for me."

Ching asked Tom, "Do you want to do *real* construction?" and took his nephew to the laborers union and arranged to have him join Hawaiian Dredging & Construction for the summer.

"Instead of joining my cousins, I worked on the H-1 freeway," said Tom, smiling. "He had a different vision for me. I was indebted to him because that really taught me what hard, physical work was all about. It also motivated me not to screw up. I did the best I could, and I think it turned out pretty well."

Tom followed Ching's advice to go to law school. "I thought business school sounded better for me, but he pointed me in another direction," said Tom. "He said that you become a better businessman through life experiences, but in law you have to go through a regimented program to become a professional. He told me that you can do business with a law degree and legal background, but you cannot practice law with a business degree. And he was right about that."

Added Tom, "I was impressed with how someone can be so influential without being at the forefront. Clarence was able to lead from the side or from the back. I learned that this is an incredibly effective trait. You do not have to be the drum major to be a leader. People will follow you because you are competent, you care and you are a success—and Clarence was certainly all of that."

Wendell Lew, another nephew, said that Ching always expected more from his family.

"He was very demanding," said Lew, who worked for his uncle as a property manager before moving into the mortgage business. "If you worked for him, he expected more from you. I had to work extra hard because other people thought I would goof off."

Lew admired Ching for being a man of his word. "When he was selling off lots at Salt Lake, people would ask him if they could purchase lots at favorable prices. Even years later, when people came back to him and said, 'You promised me this lot at this price,' he would honor his word, even if there was nothing in writing.

"Clarence was a self-made man who had a special knack for recognizing a good deal. He could see the potential in things, and he could convince people to trust his vision. People had confidence in him, and that is a big reason why he was so successful." &

In the 1970s, Lakeside was notable as one of Hawai`i's few
fee-simple subdivisions.

In the summer of 1965, Clarence addressed a crowd of more than 700
at a ceremonial *lūʻau* for Lakeside on the shores of Salt Lake. Opposite top:
At the lake's center, Ching, *kahuna* David Bray and Pat Carscadden of
Hawaiian Dredging & Construction Company make an offering to the gods.
Opposite bottom: Bray leads the *imu* ceremony, accompanied by dignitaries
including Clarence (far right) and Honolulu Mayor Neal Blaisdell (fifth from left).

The Chinese Cultural Plaza made its debut in January 1975 with festivities including traditional dances on the Moongate Stage (opposite top).

CULTURAL PLAZA
MOONGATE STAGE

ASIA TRAVEL

Still under construction in early 1970 (top),
Kukui Gardens welcomed its first tenants in May of that year.

Clarence and Gov. John A. Burns present ceremonial keys to
Kukui Gardens' first tenants.

Clarence T.C. Ching was an associate and confidant of many Island political leaders, including U.S. Sen. Hiram L. Fong and Gov. John A. Burns.

CHAPTER SIX

KUKUI GARDENS

KUKUI GARDENS

Thirty minutes. For Clarence Ching, that short length of time was the difference between building the crown jewel of his professional life and missing out on the opportunity altogether.

In 1966, the Honolulu Redevelopment Agency (HRA), in conjunction with the Department of Housing and Urban Development (HUD), invited individual developers and organizations to submit proposals for a long-anticipated and much-needed affordable housing complex. The project involved approximately 19.5 acres of land on a tract at Vineyard Boulevard and Liliha Street. The site had been vacant, covered only with weeds, since bulldozers had brought down hundreds of dilapidated, termite-ridden houses some five years earlier.

Identified simply as "The Kukui Project, Hawaii No. R-2," the plan called for no fewer than 800 apartment units built for low- and moderate-income families.

This was at a time when most Hawai'i developers were focusing on building big-dollar hotels and residential communities in the state's affluent areas. While low-income housing was sorely needed, it was simply not as profitable as other developments.

By this time in his life, Ching was already widely recognized as a well-respected and successful developer and businessman. He had earned enough wealth to provide for his family.

"He was never money hungry," recalled his longtime attorney and friend, George Hong. "He had enough money. Now, he was looking for a way to give back."

This HRA project, Ching felt, was the opportunity to do just that.

Only two non-profit organizations submitted proposals on November 24, 1966. One was from the Hawaii Council for Housing Action (HCHA), a group that included the International Longshoremen & Workers Union, Oceanic Properties, Alexander & Baldwin and the Honolulu Council of Churches. The other was from the still-to-be-established Clarence T.C. Ching Foundation.

The HCHA was almost awarded the project by default. Because Ching and his collaborators were so determined to win over the HRA, they put much time and effort into their proposal. As a result, according to HRA Director Lee Maice, the Ching Foundation's proposal did not arrive until 11:30 a.m., a scant 30 minutes before the noon deadline.

The HCHA plan called for a 778-unit development with monthly rents ranging from $100 to $165. The average rent would be $135.19 a month. The plan suggested a combination of low-rise buildings with three- and four-bedroom units for large families and towers for one- and two-bedroom units for smaller families and the elderly.

Ching's plan included an 832-unit complex with rents ranging from $77 to $155 a month. Under his proposal, the average monthly rent would be $116.01. Ching's vision called for one-, two-, three- and four-bedroom apartments clustered together in a "row or townhouse concept."

Projections for each proposal carried an estimated price tag of just under $15 million, not including the purchase price of the land.

Said Lee Maice to *Honolulu Advertiser* reporter Bill Cook: "It appears that much thought and planning has gone into both submissions."

By rule, the HRA had 60 days to look over the proposals before selecting the winning bid.

On December 12, representatives from the competing parties presented their cases in person at a public hearing. About 60 people attended the 90-minute session held inside a Honolulu Police Department meeting room. César Pelli of Daniel, Mann, Johnson & Mendenhall, the architectural and planning firm that helped prepare the proposal for Ching's group, told those in attendance that their plan was designed "for people," adding that tenants would enjoy a feeling "of belonging" instead of being just another apartment number in another housing project.

A hint of the way the HRA was leaning was given at a January 5, 1967, meeting. Wrote Mike Fern of the *Honolulu Star-Bulletin*: "The Ching proposal appears to have the edge on operating costs and monthly rentals. And because it has more units, it seems to have a better distribution of the various sizes … Douglas Myers, a Mainland consultant to the HRA, said the Ching plan has lower rentals and operating costs, but offers more accessories."

Finally, on January 19, Ching received the good news: The HRA had officially awarded him the Kukui housing contract. HRA Vice Chair Donald S. Umemoto listed four reasons for selecting Ching: "1) the proposed development is well designed; 2) it will offer private housing to moderate-income families at the lowest possible rents consistent with good design; 3) the developer is experienced and financially responsible; and 4) his proposal meets all objectives stated by the [HRA] agency in its original brochure."

"He was so thrilled!" Hong recounted. "He really wanted the Kukui project. I remember Stuart Ho [an attorney, developer and businessman] calling me and asking, 'What is this? Is this for real? What is the catch?' But there was no catch. Clarence was serious about doing this for the community."

The development would be called Kukui Gardens.

The next step for Ching was to form his non-profit foundation, which would serve as the sponsor for the project. The Clarence T.C. Ching Foundation was officially created, via trust agreement, on August 8, 1967. The five charter Trustees were Henry C.H. Chun-Hoon, head of Chun-Hoon Markets; Jasper J. Jepson, Secretary and Vice President of Bishop Trust Company; Dr. Katsumi Kometani, a dentist; Ralph M. Miwa, a political science professor at the University of Hawai'i; and Clarence Ching himself, who funded the trust with an initial contribution of $10,000 in cash.

On August 25, 1967, the State of Hawai'i's Director of Regulatory Agencies issued a Charter of Incorporation establishing the non-profit Kukui Gardens Corporation to purchase and develop the 19.5-acre parcel in downtown Honolulu. That group would include the five Clarence T.C. Ching Foundation Trustees, five members from Chaminade University's Board of Regents and five members of St. Francis Medical Center's Lay Advisory Board. Ching would serve as President of the Kukui Gardens Corporation.

A week later, in a September 2 *Honolulu Advertiser* account, the HRA's Maice praised Ching "for electing to use the same organizational skills and business acumen that made him a nationally important land developer to produce, without profit, homes for families in our community that cannot compete at the cost demanded by today's market. Producing homes is a complicated business. The skill and imagination of those who have made a success of it ... are needed to solve the problems of housing for our moderate-income families.... The formula devised by Mr. Ching is a product of his unique abilities. I am hopeful that this formula will be followed by others with unique abilities."

The Foundation was expected to be perpetual. Under government regulations, earnings from the housing project needed to be kept in a residential fund, to be periodically used to reduce rentals. "This means," the *Advertiser*'s Bill Cook wrote, "it could be forty years—when the development mortgage is paid off—before revenue for charity is derived for such stated purposes as assisting the needy, sick and aged."

Right away, Ching put up $400,000 of his own money to secure a loan from Bank of Hawai'i for initial working capital for the project. Construction on Kukui Gardens, he added, would begin as soon as eight months.

In June 1968, Kukui Gardens Corporation submitted its final plans for the project: Kukui Gardens would have 105 one-bedroom units, 302 two-bedroom units, 279 three-bedroom units and 136 four-bedroom units—a total of 822 apartment units. The complex would feature four six-story buildings with elevators as well as three-story townhouse structures. A separate day care center and recreation building would also be built for use by all Kukui Gardens tenants.

Financing for the project would come from The Ford Foundation, which would lend Kukui Gardens Corporation the sum of $16.1 million. That amount would be secured by a mortgage of the project property, insured by the Federal Housing Administration Commissioner. (Under the provisions of the National Housing Act, the FHA Commissioner is authorized to insure mortgages made for the purposes of purchasing, constructing and operating rental projects for families of low and moderate income.)

"Public officials who have had to rationalize the slowness of the urban renewal process are almost openly jubilant that the valuable, idle land is about to be used," the *Advertiser's* Cook wrote.

Of course, with any construction project of this magnitude, setbacks were bound to occur, and Kukui Gardens was no different.

The first occurred in the late summer of 1968. The initial construction work had been scheduled to start on August 1, but unforeseen cost problems necessitated a slight delay. The FHA explained that soil tests had shown that stronger footings were needed for many of the proposed structures. As a result, additional financing was required. The new target date to begin construction was around the middle of November.

November came and went. On December 12, a *Honolulu Advertiser* article noted that January 14 was set as the closing date on the property, and construction work could begin the following day. It was not until February, however, that work on the project was finally underway.

At least a few interested observers were getting anxious. The *Honolulu Adver-*

tiser reported that the HRA "has been the butt of much criticism because the former residents of the rundown area were moved out and the whole property bulldozed. Then for five years it sat vacant."

Nevertheless, concern gave way to happy smiles on Tuesday, February 11, when ground was broken for Kukui Gardens. A number of public officials attended the special ceremony, including Senator Hiram Fong and Mayor Frank Fasi. As part of the festivities, Ching planted a kukui tree at the corner of Liliha and King Streets.

Noted the *Advertiser* the following day, "The breaking of ground for a new construction project is normally the occasion for the usual superlatives—praising the greatness of the project, the vision of the developer and the benefit to mankind that will result from the completed structure. But although the groundbreaking ceremony for the $16-million Kukui Gardens moderate-income apartment development yesterday was liberally sprinkled with just those phrases, no one could overcome the feeling of relief that the project finally was getting under way.

"In fact, Mayor Frank F. Fasi expressed it all by saying, 'It's about time!'"

Among the honored guests at the ceremony were Mr. and Mrs. Simplicio Veto. The Vetos were residents of the old Kukui area before being evicted for the redevelopment project in 1962.

"I cried when I had to move, because I knew I would miss [my friends]," the 51-year-old Mrs. Veto told a reporter. "There was never any trouble in the neighborhood. Everyone got along just like one family."

Now, the Vetos were among the first people scheduled to become tenants of Kukui Gardens.

Said Fasi, "I hope to see—I intend to see—more housing developed of this type in Honolulu, and without the need to displace people for whom there is no comparable replacement housing available." To the crowd's approval, Fasi recited an old Greek proverb: "If you would make your city loved, you must first make her lovable."

About two years later, however, as construction on Kukui Gardens was drawing to a close, Fasi was whistling a different tune.

A few critics of the project began complaining about the closely packed, boxed-in look of the new complex. Said one public official, "We are in the process of creating another noisy and unpleasant slum." At one point, Fasi, an arch-nemesis of the HRA, even considered putting a stop to the construction.

George Hong, Ching's attorney, explained that the high density of the layout was due to the HRA's requirement that 800 units be built on the 19.5 acres.

Added Melvin Shinn of the HRA: "When you talk of this kind of rental, you're not going to get all the amenities. We're talking dollars and cents. If you spent $40,000 per unit, you wouldn't be able to rent it for $77 a month."

The criticism, however, never amounted to much. More telling was the fact that more than 1,000 applications had been filed for the 822 apartments. Even after the units were filled, there would be some 3,000 additional applications for apartments that might be vacated later.

In late May of 1970, the time for talk was over. Finally, it was time for Kukui Gardens to welcome its first tenants.

On May 28, Gov. John A. Burns presented sets of apartment keys to several of the first families scheduled to move into the housing complex. Among the recipients were Mr. and Mrs. Veto.

"This is an outstanding example of how human needs can be met through government action, followed by private initiative, energy and know-how," Burns said. "Too frequently, we find people prone to use genuine human needs for political demagoguery—for easy generalizations about what is wrong in housing, or in this or in that. Who is to quarrel with success, except those who seem to take comfort in finding fault even with the 'Second Coming'?"

(Mayor Fasi, who was not present at the dedication, later heard about the "demagoguery" comment. "I don't know who made the remark," he fired back, "but it sounds like an idiot who is running for office again this year.")

Honolulu City Council Chairman Walter Heen also voiced his appreciation for Kukui Gardens. "Certainly it cannot be said that this project is the best designed in the world," he said in a prepared speech. "But, when landscaped and painted, it may not be the worst design in the world."

Later, after taking a tour of the units, Heen smiled and added, "And, in fact, it may come close to being the best designed."

Like the Vetos, Mr. and Mrs. Richard Park and their four children were also former residents of the area. They were also among the first to receive their keys to their new Kukui Gardens unit.

"There is so much space and privacy," marveled Richard Park to a reporter. "For the first time in my life, I'll be able to do yard work. I always wanted to have a yard."

Even the news media seemed to revel in the occasion. *Honolulu Star-Bulletin* scribe Phil Mayer wrote, "The worst part of it used to be called 'Hell's Half Acre.' It used to be Honolulu's worst downtown slum. About 5,000 people used to live here. But for seven years—from 1962 to 1969—it was a 20-acre, weed-dotted bulldozed wasteland visited only by the wind.

"Today, it is a community which has come back to life."

In his speech dedicating the opening of Kukui Gardens, Ching expressed his gratitude to the project's general contractor, Hawaiian Dredging & Construction Company. "I submit that Hawaiian Dredging's demonstrated cooperation refutes the commonly entertained proposition that a profit-motivated contractor is incapable of contributing to the social welfare of the community," he asserted.

Ching also took a shot at critics of the project, saying, "It troubles me that so many people are prone to criticize without offering solutions. We—all of us—have at least tried." True to form, however, the humble Ching added that dissent and criticism should not only be tolerated, but encouraged.

A special luncheon was held to celebrate the occasion. The Parks and Vetos were among the guests who dined on filet mignon and listened to the day's speeches. Guests at the head table included Ching; Governor Burns; Walter Heen; Ching Foundation Trustee Ralph Miwa; Alvin Pang, the Hawai'i District Director of the FHA; George Wheaton, President of Dillingham Corporation; Dillingham Vice President Herb Cornuelle; Irwin Mendenhall, President of Daniel, Mann, Johnson & Mendenhall; HRA Commissioner Joseph Lunasco; Karen Goldfarb, "Miss HUD"; and Rev. Robert Mackey, Chancellor of the Saint Louis-Chaminade Education Center.

The following week, HRA acting manager Melvin Shinn penned an editorial that appeared in the June 10 edition of the *Honolulu Advertiser*.

"I doubt that there is a single person in our State that is not aware that the cost of housing is the major problem our State, and especially the City and County of Honolulu, faces today," Shinn stated. "But despite this basic knowledge, apparently, none of the 'authorities' who have decried the Kukui housing project have, in forming and expressing their opinions, taken this into consideration.

"You don't have to be an expert to realize that, indeed, a 'better' plan … a more beautiful design … a more luxurious concept could have been achieved for the Kukui Project. The HRA, in fact, did investigate other schemes. The insurmountable barrier? The dollar.

"I have noticed that, as the Kukui Gardens Housing Project draws nearer to completion, the volume and severity of criticism directed at it has lessened considerably. Could it be that the critics realize that it would be more difficult to find sympathetic ears for their derisive comments now that the project is out of the 'concrete shell' stage and is no longer the eyesore that, in fact, all projects are in the early stages of their development?

"Do they foresee that once the landscaping is completed at Kukui Gardens, once the adjacent six-acre park is completed, adding its beauty to the overall project, once 822 families move into their new homes, at rents ranging from $84.50 for one-bedroom to $146 for four-bedroom apartments (a housing situation that a multitude of our residents would love to be in), that their cries of 'bad planning' and 'concrete jungle' would fall on deaf ears?"

There would be more vindication to come. Imagine critics of Kukui Gardens waking up on November 15, 1970, opening up their Sunday newspaper and seeing the headline: "Kukui Gardens project wins national award."

Yes, less than four months after officially welcoming its first tenants, Kukui Gardens was cited by the American Institute of Architects (AIA) and its sponsoring agencies. A jury of experts studied 78 entries in the national design competition before selecting Daniel, Mann, Johnson & Mendenhall, the project's designers.

"This no-nonsense, yet attractive, solution gives every tenant a street address," the jury noted. "The piggyback principle allows density of forty-two percent per acre on thirty percent coverage. It affords on-site perimeter parking and exhibits a healthy disdain for fashionable clichés in current urban design."

The project's architect, César Pelli, would go on to design some of the world's tallest and most recognized structures, including the Petronas Twin Towers in Malaysia, the World Financial Center complex in New York, the Wells Fargo Center in Minnesota and the Bank of America Corporate Center in North Carolina. In 1991, the AIA named Pelli as "one of the ten most influential living American architects." He was also honored with an AIA Gold Medal, which recognizes a body of work of lasting influence on the theory and practice of architecture.

Kukui Gardens was honored again in July of 1971, when it was one of 21 award winners in the AIA's annual Homes for Better Living program. The project's design earned acclaim in *House & Home* and *American Home* magazines, which helped sponsor the design competition.

In 2002, Kukui Gardens received another commendation, this time from

HUD, as one of the best housing projects in the country.

The best and most important judges, of course, were the tenants themselves. More than fifteen years after Kukui Gardens had its public unveiling, *Honolulu Star-Bulletin* writer Jerry Tune visited the housing project. There, he met fifteen-year tenant Helen Ebia.

"It is a wonderful place," said Ebia in the *Star-Bulletin*'s June 15, 1986, feature. "My husband and I raised our children here. They are grown now, but they return often to visit. They like to come back.

"It's very safe here. We have good security and residents respect each other. There was, from the start, a sense of family throughout the project and it is still here today."

Added Angie Among, property manager and one of the original occupants at Kukui Gardens: "Our rents have always been low. People feel very fortunate to live here. Many people have lived here, saved money, and then went on to buy a home or condominium. Many of these people come back and tell me, 'Thanks for helping me save.'"

In his 35-year career as a developer, Clarence Ching helped create thousands of residential units for Hawai'i's people. There is little doubt, however, that the 822-unit Kukui Gardens project gave him the most personal satisfaction.

As George Hong said, "That was Clarence's pride and joy."

In 1966, when asked why he was interested in the Kukui project, Ching explained that the development would give him a vehicle for setting up a charitable trust.

"I have been blessed with good fortune in this community," he said. "I consider the Kukui project an opportunity to discharge this obligation." ❧

CHAPTER SEVEN
THE BAMBOO
PROVERB

THE BAMBOO PROVERB

For Gene Tiwanak, Clarence Ching was more than a business associate. He was even more than a friend or mentor.

"I was playing golf one day at Moanalua Golf Course," said Tiwanak. "This was in the early 1980s. Playing the hole ahead of me was a woman and her little kid. Well, I hit the ball, and I thought it was one of my best drives. It carried the ravine. I yelled, 'Fore!' But the ball hit their cart. I went up to her to apologize. Man, she was angry! I mean, she was just livid! She kept yelling at me, and maybe rightly so. Finally, she blurted out, 'Do you know who I am? I am Mrs. Damon!'

"I thought, 'Uh oh.' I had no idea what to say. I was stunned.

"Finally, I just said the first thing that came to my mind," he continued. "I said, 'And do you know who *I* am?' I really took her aback. She said, 'No. Who are you?' And I joked and said, 'I'm Clarence Ching's son!'

"Then I turned around and jumped back into my cart! Later on, I told Clarence what had happened, and he just laughed and laughed. He thought it was hilarious! Afterward, every time we were out someplace, he would ask me to tell people that story."

Clarence Ching had a way of making everyone feel like family.

Ching had always been very conscious of his health, even to the point of seeking chelation therapy, the sometimes-controversial blood-cleansing treatment designed to treat or prevent the hardening of the arteries.

Nevertheless, in 1985 Ching's doctors discovered a problem with his heart. It was recommended that he undergo bypass surgery. Ching refused.

"He thought he could beat it with medication and exercise," recalled his nephew Ray Tam.

"He was in the hospital," said his younger brother Herbert, "but he asked to be discharged. He did not want to stay there, so he got out."

On Wednesday, May 29, Ching was playing golf at the Waialae Country Club. After teeing off at the 12th hole, he suddenly felt ill. He sat down on the ground, then fell backwards.

In the group behind Ching's was Dr. Ichiro Nadamoto, an orthopaedic specialist and family friend. He raced over to the fallen Ching and gave him CPR but could not revive him.

Clarence T.C. Ching, Hawai'i's humble humanitarian, was dead. He was 72.

"In a way, it was a blessing, because he died without any kind of pain," said Tam. "He never suffered."

"Developer Clarence T.C. Ching Dies at 72," the May 31 *Honolulu Star-Bulletin* announced. The lead paragraph read, "Clarence T.C. Ching, who turned large tracts of Honolulu into housing and industrial parks, died Wednesday in Queen's Hospital after a heart attack while playing golf at Waialae Country Club."

That same day, the *Honolulu Advertiser* reported: "Clarence T.C. Ching, a Honolulu developer and financial executive once described by associates as 'a doer, not a talker,' died Wednesday of a heart attack while playing golf at Waialae Country Club. He would have been 73 on Sunday."

The *Advertiser* later paid tribute to Ching in a June 5 editorial: "Clarence T.C. Ching, who died Wednesday at age 72, was a quiet man—but he had vision, a belief in hard work and a strong commitment to the welfare of his community.… He was a builder, both literally and in the broadest sense of the word. He constructed an industrial park, countless apartments and a non-profit complex of rental housing for more than 800 low- and moderate-income families—to mention only some of his projects.

"But for him money meant something beyond personal accumulation. He established a foundation whose primary beneficiaries are St. Louis-Chaminade Educational Center and St. Francis Hospital. He gave time, energy and assistance to many other organizations.

"We at the *Advertiser* know this first-hand, for he was one of the earliest supporters of the Contemporary Arts Center. When its first director, Violet Yap, asked him in 1961 to help fund the initial improvements to the *Advertiser*'s central court, since the newspaper was then not financially able to do so, he responded immediately.… He and a few of his friends contributed everything that was needed in money and materials, including the bronze letters which he personally approved and which to this day are located above the museum's entrance.

"As the son of an immigrant father, Clarence Ching worked hard all his life. He proved that a humble beginning is no barrier if one has constructive dreams and the ability and determination to make them come true.

"His good deeds will live after him. But he will be sorely missed by all who knew him and of his deep care for this community."

Clarence Ching's memorial service was held on Saturday, June 8, 1985, at Diamond Head Memorial Park. Father Robert R. Mackey, S.M., one of the founders and the first President of Chaminade University in Honolulu, presented the eulogy. Here is an excerpt:

This afternoon we remember in simple religious rites a humble and unpretentious man who emerged as a giant in the new springtime of Hawai'i. We gather also to assure Dorothy, his widow, and his children Larry, Wally and Jocelyn that we co-agonize with them at this time of loss and that we join them in pilgrimage that will unite us one day with Clarence. All of us present here have individually offered condolences to members of the extended Ching family for whom Clarence, the eldest surviving member, had provided; and at this moment in our rites, we express our concern as a community with a single voice.

Clarence was in his 72nd year when he returned his life to the Creator on the golf links of Waialae on Wednesday, May 29. In a short while we, his family and friends, will confide his mortal remains to the earth of the Memorial Park where he will rest in the company of more than thirty Brothers of Mary, his teachers and the teachers of his brothers, children and grandchildren at Saint Louis College.

All his life Clarence was faithful to the lessons of the priority of family and community that he learned from the example of his immigrant father at the family rice farm and mill on the island of Kaua'i. He learned that the individual grows in value as he serves the family and the community. Years before our 35th President of the United States stated this basic religious truth in his inaugural address on January 20, 1961, Clarence was exemplifying it. John F. Kennedy said: "My fellow Americans: Ask not what your country can do for you—ask what you can do for your country." A strong voice rooted in Chinese traditions and in Clarence's soul cried out to him continually: "Ask not what your community can do for you—ask what you can do for your community."

He left the family farm on Kaua'i in September 1928 to become a freshman at Saint Louis College at the new location of Kaimukī. He felt at home with the Brothers of Mary who shared his values of the priority of family and community. During four years there, he was twice president of his class. He was initiated into CLIA—the Chinese Literary Improvement Association—an honorary society of Chinese students with a scholastic average of 85 percent or more, for improving and stimulating the members along literary lines, especially in the betterment of English.

He regretted that he was unable to complete a post-secondary academic degree, but he remained associated with Saint Louis College and then Chaminade University all his life and received [a degree] in humane letters, honoris causa, *from Chaminade.*

He expressed belief in Church-related education by serving in various capacities on the Board of Trustees and the Board of Directors of the Saint Louis-Chaminade Education Center and the Board of Regents of Chaminade University. I was closely associated with Clarence during those years and observed firsthand his authentic, unfeigned humility; his self-effacement; his respect for every person; his patient listening and his ability to discern the critical issues and to collaborate in planning and action.

I left those meetings with Clarence with a new sense of my own personal worth and the importance of the community project that brought us together. It was a personal privilege to be associated with Clarence in the new springtime in the life of Hawai'i as immigrant groups and Native Hawaiians emerged as significant actors in all aspects of our community life. In politics it was the new Democratic Party under the leadership of the late John A. Burns, who counted Clarence among his trusted counselors. In the cultural life of Honolulu, it was the Chinese Cultural Plaza across the stream from the Kukui Gardens and also the Contemporary Arts Center.

With his classmate, K.J. Luke, he was a co-founder of the Hawaii National Bank and offered the community a whole array of financial services; and later he became a principal stockholder in Liberty Bank.

We are all aware of the place of Dynamic Industries and the various functions of Loyalty Enterprises in the growth of the new Hawai'i, ranging from the industrial park at the International Airport to the hundreds of family dwellings in the Salt Lake and Moanalua areas.

Clarence was especially proud of the Kukui Gardens Project that provides rental housing for more than 800 low- and moderate-income families. The United States Department of Housing and Urban Development awarded special honors to this project for excellence in design, construction and management. I urge you to visit this memorial to Clarence and read the inscription on the plaque at the stream side near Beretania Street:

Kukui Gardens
Dedicated February 11, 1969
Kukui Gardens Corporation
The Clarence T.C. Ching Foundation
It was with usual modesty and with great reluctance that Clarence allowed his

name to be given to the foundation. He preferred "The Kukui Gardens Foundation." It is the only place where his name appears as a legacy in all his endeavors for the community.

He always considered the charitable foundation and Kukui Gardens his greatest accomplishment and his special gift to the community—it became a paradigm for low- and moderate-income family housing and, at the same time, it named as sole beneficiaries the Saint Louis-Chaminade Education Center and St. Francis Hospital.

For many years Clarence was a member of the Advisory Board of St. Francis Hospital, which has pioneered family and community medical care in Hawai'i. The day before his death, he attended a meeting of the Board.

Sister Maureen of St. Francis Hospital applied to Clarence at a recent meeting of the Saint Louis-Chaminade Education Center Board meeting a conviction that she has about her veteran Franciscan Sisters. She calls them the giants on whose shoulders we build. And she said about Clarence: "He is one of those giants on whose shoulders we must continue to build."

The Chinese proverb about the bamboo expresses my reflections and describes Clarence. The Chinese say that the bamboo is the symbol of the just and righteous person—it grows tall and because it is hollow, it is strong and flexible. The just and righteous person grows tall in the community, and because he is empty of all selfishness, he is strong and he bends in the service of others.

I conclude this eulogy with that thought. Our presence this afternoon is an affirmation of our own belief in the priority of family and community, the values that Clarence cherished. We are called to continue to build our beautiful community and our families on the shoulders of Clarence, the strong, humble, quiet, self-effacing and generous giant—the just and righteous one.

• • •

Ching's legacy would live on through his family. His beloved wife, Dorothy, lived for another six years before succumbing to Parkinson's disease. She passed away in May 1991.

Their oldest son, Larry, became the youngest President of a Hawai'i bank when he took the helm of Liberty Bank in 1975. A graduate of Saint Louis School and Washington University in St. Louis, Missouri, he was also past President of the Hawaii Bankers Association; President of the Chinese Chamber of Commerce; a

Above: In 1982 Clarence and Dorothy pose with their family at Dorothy's
71st birthday celebration at the Hilton Hawaiian Village.
Top: Clarence and bankers finalize financing for the development of
700 lots in the Moanalua Golf Course subdivision.

Clarence T.C. Ching Foundation grants have supported a number of Hawai`i's educational institutions, including the University of Hawai`i-Mānoa's Clarence T.C. Ching Athletic Complex (top), the Clarence T.C. Ching Learning and Technology Center at Saint Louis School (above) and Clarence T.C. Ching Hall at Chaminade University (opposite).

CLARENCE T.C. CHING HALL
MARIANIST CENTER OF HAWAII

Maryknoll School completed its Clarence T.C. Ching Gymnasium with a $3-million donation from the Foundation.

Damien Memorial High School students celebrate the announcement that The Clarence T.C. Ching Foundation will provide tuition aid grants to financially challenged students. Above: A $2-million grant provided funding for a new three-floor structure at the Palolo Chinese Home.

Top: A $5-million grant made it possible for Catholic Charities Hawai`i
to purchase and renovate its 2.2-acre Makiki campus.
Above: Sacred Hearts Academy built a new dance studio at its
Performing Arts Center with a $150,000 grant.

A $3-million contribution helped fund Punahou School's PUEO program (Partners in Unlimited Educational Opportunities). Top: Foundation Trustees present a check to school President Jim Scott and Punahou Board Chairman Warren Luke.

At Hanahauoli School, a $1-million grant helps support the Professional Development Center program, which promotes education with an emphasis on experience-based learning. Top (right to left.): The Clarence T.C. Ching Foundation President R. Stevens Gilley and Trustees Peter P.J. Ng, Treasurer; Chairman John K. Tsui; Vice Chairman Raymond J. Tam; Catherine H.Q. Ching, Secretary; and Kenneth T. Okamoto.

member of Chaminade University's Board of Regents; a Trustee of The Clarence T.C. Ching Foundation; and President of Kukui Gardens Corporation.

Larry was also active in the community, serving as Director of the Hawaii Heart Association; Director and Treasurer of Aloha United Way; and Lay Advisory Board Member for St. Francis Medical Center. An avid sports enthusiast, he was a dedicated fan of University of Hawai'i sports and was a member of both the Honolulu Country Club and Waialae Country Club.

Larry and his wife, Frances "Mimi" Ching, had four children. Larry died on August 21, 2007, at the age of 71.

Wallace S.J. Ching parlayed his degrees at USC, the Northwestern University School of Law and Harvard Business School into a highly successful career in the State Attorney General's office. He also served as President of Loyalty Enterprises, was a Director at Kukui Gardens Corporation and was a Trustee of The Clarence T.C. Ching Foundation.

He was also President of the Building Industry Association-Hawaii; President of the Chinese Chamber of Commerce; President of the United Chinese Society and Organization of Chinese Americans-Hawaii; and Director of the Marianist Center of Hawaii, the Honolulu Symphony Society and Bishop Museum.

In 2008, Wallace was named an "Unsung Hero" by the Organization of Chinese Americans.

He remains a Director at Loyalty Development.

He and his former wife, Edna, have two children. He is married to Ann Suzuki.

Clarence's youngest child, Jocelyn Ching, has served her family as a dedicated homemaker and housewife. She and her husband, Clifford, have four children.

Although he did not openly express it, Clarence Ching dearly loved his family and friends. And the feeling was always mutual. Gene Tiwanak remembered the times he would see his friend full of joy: "At Christmas, I would get a phone call from Dorothy [Tam Ching], his secretary. And she would tell me, 'Mr. Ching would like to see you, and please bring Sister Maureen Keleher.' So we would go to see him—sometimes it was at Loyalty, and sometimes it was at Hawaii National Bank—and there would be Clarence and K.J. [Luke]. They would walk up to us and give us a check for $50,000 or $60,000! I would look at Clarence, and he would be smiling from ear to ear.

"He was always so giving, so generous. He always thought of others. That is just the kind of man he was." ❧

CHAPTER EIGHT

LEGACY

LEGACY

Clarence Ching is gone, but the Foundation he started more than 40 years ago—The Clarence T.C. Ching Foundation—still carries on his vision of helping people in need.

In the years following Ching's passing, the Foundation did what it could to support Hawai'i's non-profit agencies and educational institutions, using money collected from revenues from rent and parking fees at Kukui Gardens. In December 1996, for example, the Foundation made a $250,000 pledge contribution to Chaminade University. In the summer of 1999, an additional $175,000 was donated to the school for a new computer classroom and conference center. Contributions were also made to Saint Louis School to fund the Clarence T.C. Ching Scholar awards, as well as St. Francis Medical Center and other local organizations.

But members of the Foundation felt that more could be done to follow Ching's mission of giving. On January 11, 2006, the Foundation announced that it was seeking a buyer for the Kukui Gardens housing complex. It was explained that the non-profit Foundation could no longer afford to run Kukui Gardens. Furthermore, selling the complex would ensure the continued viability of the Foundation and enable it to expand its charitable giving. And according to Foundation Spokesperson R. Stevens Gilley, the timing for the sale was right, as housing and land prices had been skyrocketing in the midst of a robust construction boom on O'ahu.

Kukui Gardens' 40-year mortgage agreement with the U.S. Department of Housing and Urban Development (HUD) was set to expire in 2011. "Kukui Gardens was never intended go on forever," explained Clarence T.C. Ching Foundation Trustee Peter Ng. "Clarence's intent from day one was that funds from the project would one day benefit the entire community."

The news of the sale attracted seventeen prospective buyers. By mid-March, that list was narrowed down to three finalists. Commercial real estate services company CB Richard Ellis was handling the sale, working under the direction of R. Stevens Gilley.

Not unexpectedly, many Kukui Gardens tenants protested the move. They were concerned that the new owner might go around the HUD agreement and find a way to evict them before 2011. A petition was created, asking HUD for assurance that the current owner, Kukui Gardens Corporation, and any future owner would keep rents affordable.

Whoever the buyer turned out to be, Gilley assured the tenants, "They're not going to evict anybody. They want the tenants there." Later, the Kukui Gardens Board released an official statement: "The owners of Kukui Gardens have repeatedly stressed to the leadership of the Kukui Gardens Tenants Association that they have no intention of accepting an offer from a buyer who will evict the current tenants and raze the complex."

Potential buyers, the statement continued, would be required to meet three criteria: readily available financing, approval from HUD and assurances that "the buyer intends to continue managing the housing complex as it is today."

Complicating matters was a *Honolulu Star-Bulletin* report that State lawmakers were considering a bill that would condemn Kukui Gardens to keep it as affordable housing.

"People were saying that selling Kukui Gardens was never Clarence's intent," recalled Peter Ng, who sat on the Kukui Gardens Board. "But that *was* his intent. That had been the whole plan from the start. In his vision of housing development in Hawai'i, Kukui Gardens was just one portion of that vision. He never tried to hold on to it and say, 'We need to keep this intact.' Never."

"Kukui Gardens was started to subsidize the low- to moderate-income people, the immigrants, to give them a home for 40 years," explained Herbert Ching. "Once people had the cheap rent, of course, they did not want to move out. But you cannot subsidize a certain group of people for life. That was not the original intent."

In April, Carmel Partners Inc., a private real estate firm based in San Francisco that had extensive experience in low- to moderate-income housing developments, emerged as the leading candidate to purchase Kukui Gardens. Representatives from the firm met privately with the tenants to allay fears of higher rents or evictions. The head of the Kukui Gardens Tenants Association called the meeting "positive."

Finally, an agreement was reached in January 2007 that essentially divided Kukui Gardens in two, with one half sold to Carmel Partners and the other half to the State of Hawai'i for continued use as affordable housing for tenants.

"As we have said all along, Carmel is the best hope for continued affordable rentals at Kukui Gardens because they have the resources to implement much-needed repairs and maintenance, as well as the experience to successfully manage the property," Kukui Gardens Corporation officials said in a statement.

The sale became official in December 2007, with the purchase price announced at $131 million. *Pacific Business News* would later call it "the biggest Hawai'i real estate deal" of 2007-08, beating out the sales of such properties as Ocean View Court, Haseko Center, the Gold Bond Building and the Park Shore Waikiki Hotel.

• • •

It did not take long for The Clarence T.C. Ching Foundation to put some of the proceeds from the Kukui Gardens sale to good use.

In May 2008, the Foundation donated $5 million to the University of Hawai'i Athletic Department. School officials called it the largest single donation ever made to UH athletics. The money would be used to refurbish Cooke Field, which was subsequently renamed the Clarence T.C. Ching Field. The field was resurfaced in 2008, including future plans calling for seating for up to 3,500 spectators, locker rooms, offices, storage areas, a press box and a scoreboard.

"During his lifetime, Mr. Ching was a loyal fan of University of Hawai'i athletics," pointed out Jack Tsui, Trustee and Chair of the Foundation. "We believe he would be pleased that, through the Clarence T.C. Ching Field, the Foundation will be supporting team- and leadership-building programs as well as student wellness for generations to come."

Two months later, on July 8, the Foundation provided Catholic Charities Hawai'i with a $5-million grant, which would help purchase and renovate its 2.2-acre campus in Makiki. Jerry Rauckhorst, President and CEO of Catholic Charities, called the donation "unbelievable." It is the largest financial gift the agency has ever received. Said Rauckhorst, "We are honored to be a part of Clarence Ching's historical commitment to our community, and we applaud the generous support the Foundation gives for the benefit of individuals and families statewide."

In September of that year, the Foundation gave Chaminade University a $5-million grant to help repair and renovate the school's historic Freitas Hall. Termite infestation and water damage had caused a section of the hall's roof to cave in earlier in the year, causing heavy damages to the offices. In honor of the generous gift, the hall was renamed after Clarence Ching.

A month later, the Foundation gifted Maryknoll School with a $3-million donation—the school's largest gift to date—to be used toward completing its gym and community center, the Clarence T.C. Ching Gymnasium. Said former Maryknoll Athletics Director Tony Sellitto: "Praying really helps, because I never thought I'd see this day. I'd just like to thank the Ching Foundation for helping us so much."

In November 2008, the Foundation gifted the Palolo Chinese Home—Hawai'i's largest and second-oldest residential care home—with a $2-million grant for facilities expansion, including a new three-floor structure. The Palolo Chinese Home was built in 1917 to care for former plantation workers.

In December, the Foundation made a $5.2-million commitment to Saint Louis School, which would be used to build an on-campus technology, art and business center—a 27,000-square-foot building called the Clarence T.C. Ching Learning and Technology Center, including a television production studio; a Hawaiian studies program; an adult education and community outreach program; and various business, music and art classes. Money from the donation was also earmarked for scholarships.

In January 2009, Punahou School received a $3-million contribution from the Foundation to help fund the school's Clarence T.C. Ching PUEO (Partnerships in Unlimited Educational Opportunies) program at Puhahou School, which provides needy public school students the opportunity to enroll in free summer school courses at Punahou and put them on an academic track toward college.

"We were motivated to help this thriving program because of its demonstrated ability to positively shape students' lives," said Foundation Trustee Ken Okamoto. "The PUEO program provides kids the support to realize their potential for college and beyond. We are proud to build on what PUEO has already achieved."

The following month, Hanahauoli School in Makiki was gifted with a $1-million grant from the Foundation. The donation would help fund the Clarence T.C. Ching Teachers Teaching Teachers Program, which allows the experienced faculty at Hanahauoli to mentor beginning and seasoned teachers and network with those seeking to improve their program.

In March, the Foundation donated $200,000 to Damien Memorial High School to provide tuition aid grants to academically gifted but financially challenged students. In a special ceremony inside the school's gym, Foundation Trustee Peter Ng signed an oversized check for the $200,000 amount and presented it to Damien President Bernard Ho.

In late July, to help alleviate $1.2-million budget deficit, the Foundation donated

$200,000 to Hawai'i's public high schools' athletic programs. "It's important that kids be occupied and learn discipline," said Jack Tsui in announcing the donation. "[Athletics] give them a real sense of being part of something. It takes good teachers and good students, and athletics provide a core value."

The beneficiary list goes on and on: $300,000 to Star of the Sea Church for building improvements, $150,000 to Sacred Hearts Academy for the school's performance arts building's dance studio, $150,000 to St. John the Baptist School for scholarships and professional development, $50,000 to the University of Hawai'i's Newman Catholic Center for speakers and retreats, and much more.

"It is so wonderful to be able to distribute the funds where they are needed," said Peter Ng. "Catholic Charities, for example, will serve so many different needs of the community, such as the homeless, the abused, the aged and so forth. All of these different people are in need of help, and now we are in a position to provide that help."

The Clarence T.C. Ching Foundation represents one man's selfless legacy—an organization dedicated to carrying on his lifelong passion for helping people.

According to its mission statement, the Foundation's chief goals are: 1) to assist in the care of the needy, the destitute, the sick and the aged; 2) to provide scholarship aid and assistance, without regard to amount or need and in the form of grants and loans, to those people who demonstrate the capacity and desire to improve themselves or develop their capabilities, in the expectation that such persons will ultimately, by the development of their talents and the realization of their capabilities, contribute to creating a better society; 3) to provide financial grants to qualified persons, associations and institutions for research and study in all fields, including but not limited to the natural sciences, social sciences, art, literature and music for the advancement of knowledge and culture; and 4) to assist hospitals and other public charitable or educational institutions which qualify as and are treated as tax-exempt organizations, whether supported wholly or in part by private endowment or by donations or by public taxation, with monetary contributions to defray their cost of operation and other proper expenses incurred by them.

"I consider it an honor to serve on the Foundation's Board," said Cathy Ching, Clarence's granddaughter and Foundation Trustee. "When my grandfather established the Foundation, he created a broad mission statement to help the needy, poor and those who are less fortunate. Education was also important to him. He always stressed education for our future generations."

Clarence T.C. Ching, Hawai'i's humanitarian, is gone. But in so many ways, in so many places, his legacy endures. ❊

ACKNOWLEDGMENTS

The author would like to extend a warm *mahalo* to the family, friends and colleagues of Clarence T.C. Ching for their invaluable assistance. This biography would not have been possible without the support and cooperation of The Clarence T.C. Ching Foundation, its Trustees and its President, R. Stevens Gilley. Family members who contributed to this book include Bernard Ching, Cathy Ching, Dorothy Ching, Edna Ching, Gilbert Ching, Herbert Ching, Mimi Ching, Vivian Dang, Wendell Lew, Alice Lum, Raymond Tam, Maj. Gen. Stephen Tom and Myrtle Yee. The author would also like to thank Carol Hong, George Hong, Warren Luke, Peter Ng and Gene Tiwanak for their helpful insights and contributions.

ABOUT THE AUTHOR

Lance Tominaga has written extensively about Hawai'i for more than 20 years. His previous books include *The Hawai'i Sports Trivia Challenge, Catch the Dream, The Unofficial Guide to Hawai'i* and *I Did It! (My Life After Megabucks)*.